DAYS FULL OF CAVES AND TIGERS
GIORNI PIENI DI CAVERNE E DI TIGRI

Fabio Pusterla
DAYS FULL OF CAVES AND TIGERS
GIORNI PIENI DI CAVERNE E DI TIGRI

ஒ

Translated by
Simon Knight

Introduced by
Alan Brownjohn

2012

Published by Arc Publications,
Nanholme Mill, Shaw Wood Road
Todmorden OL14 6DA, UK

Original poems copyright © Fabio Pusterla 2012
Translation copyright © Simon Knight 2012
Introduction copyright © Alan Brownjohn 2012
Copyright in the present edition © Arc Publications Ltd
Design by Tony Ward
Printed in Great Britain by the MPG Books Group,
Bodmin & King's Lynn

978 1904614 82 1 (pbk)
978 1906570 21 7 (hbk)

ACKNOWLEDGEMENTS

Poems in this collection have been selected from: *Concessione all'inverno* (Bellinzona: Edizione Casagrande, 1985); *Bocksten* (Milan: Marcos y Marcos, 1989); *Le cose senza storia* (Milan: Marcos y Marcos, 1994); *Pietra sangue* (Milan: Marcos y Marcos, 1999); *Folla sommersa* (Milan: Marcos y Marcos, 2004); *Corpo stellare* (Milan: Marcos y Marcos, 2011) and are reproduced in the original Italian by kind permission of the publishers.

Cover design by Tony Ward.

This book is in copyright. Subject to statutory exception and to provision of relevant collective licensing agreements, no reproduction of any part of this book may take place without the written permission of Arc Publications.

This book has been produced with the support of the Swiss Arts Council Pro Helvetia

swiss arts council
prohelvetia

LOTTERY FUNDED

**Arc Publications 'Visible Poets' series
Editor: Jean Boase-Beier**

CONTENTS

Series Editor's Note / 9
Translator's Preface / 11
Introduction / 15

da / from
Concessione all'inverno / Concession to Winter
22 / Le parentesi • Parentheses / 23
22 / Paradiso, Caprino, Cavallino • Paradiso, Caprino, Cavallino / 23
24 / Il dronte • The Dodo / 25

da / from
Bocksten
26 / L'anguilla del Reno • The Eel of the Rhine / 27

da / from
Le cose senza storia / Things with no Past
28 / Sonno di Claudia e Nina • Claudia and Nina Sleeping / 29
28 / Sotto il giardino • Buried in the Garden / 29
34 / Tre frammenti della disdetta • Notice to Quit: Three Fragments / 35
36 / Paesaggio • Landscape / 37
40 / Nevicare (o scrivere d'inverno) • Snowing (or Writing in Winter) / 41
40 / I crocus di Evolène • Crocuses at Evolène / 41
40 / L'annegata • The Drowned Woman / 41
42 / Crespi d'Adda • Crespi d'Adda / 43
44 / Paesaggio con Moira che scrive • Landscape with Moira Writing / 45
46 / Il merlo • The Blackbird / 47
46 / Le terre emerse • Breaking Surface / 47
50 / Vatel • Vatel / 51
52 / Continente • Continente / 53

da / from
Pietra sangue
54 / I due avversari • The Two Adversaries / 55
56 / Roggia • Drainage Canal / 57

58 / Bilancio dello sperperatore • The Spendthrift Takes Stock / 59
58 / A quelli che verranno • To Those Who Come After / 59
60 / Bois de la folie • Bois de la folie / 61
64 / Movimenti ascensionali: le scale di Albogasio • Descending and Ascending: the Stairways of Albogasio / 65
68 / Tremolìo • Tremor / 69

da / from
FOLLA SOMMERSA / SUBMERGED MULTITUDE
74 / Senza titolo • Untitled / 75
74 / Due aironi • Two Herons / 75
78 / Folla sommersa • Submerged Multitude / 79
80 / Le prime fragole • First Strawberries / 81
82 / Senza imagini • Without Images / 83
82 / Lettera da Nikolajevka • Letter from Nikolajevka / 83
84 / Deposizione • Deposition / 85
86 / Giudizio universale • Last Judgement / 87
86 / Sciame in fuga • Displaced Swarm / 87
88 / Concomitanze • Concomitances / 89
90 / I giorni sono pieni di caverne e di tigri • Days Full of Caves and Tigers / 91
92 / Dopo trent'anni • Thirty Years On / 93
94 / In cammino • Moving On / 95

from / da
HEAVENLY BODY / CORPO STELLARE
98 / Con piccole ali • On Tiny Wings / 99
98 / Aprile 2006. Cartoline d'Italia • April 2006. Postcards of Italy / 99
106 / Lettere da Babel • Letters from Babel / 107
110 / Prospect Hill • Prospect Hill / 111
112 / Storie dell'armadillo • Stories of the Armadillo / 113

Notes / 126
Biographical Notes / 129

Poetry must have something in it
that is barbaric, vast and wild.

DENIS DIDEROT, 1713-1784

SERIES EDITOR'S NOTE

The 'Visible Poets' series was established in 2000, and set out to challenge the view that translated poetry could or should be read without regard to the process of translation it had undergone. Since then, things have moved on. Today there is more translated poetry available and more debate on its nature, its status, and its relation to its original. We know that translated poetry is neither English poetry that has mysteriously arisen from a hidden foreign source, nor is it foreign poetry that has silently rewritten itself in English. We are more aware that translation lies at the heart of all our cultural exchange; without it, we must remain artistically and intellectually insular.

One of the aims of the series was, and still is, to enrich our poetry with the very best work that has appeared elsewhere in the world. And the poetry-reading public is now more aware than it was at the start of this century that translation cannot simply be done by anyone with two languages. The translation of poetry is a creative act, and translated poetry stands or falls on the strength of the poet-translator's art. For this reason 'Visible Poets' publishes only the work of the best translators, and gives each of them space, in a Preface, to talk about the trials and pleasures of their work.

From the start, 'Visible Poets' books have been bilingual. Many readers will not speak the languages of the original poetry but they, too, are invited to compare the look and shape of the English poems with the originals. Those who can are encouraged to read both. Translation and original are presented side-by-side because translations do not displace the originals; they shed new light on them and are in turn themselves illuminated by the presence of their source poems. By drawing the readers' attention to the act of translation itself, it is the aim of these books to make the work of both the original poets and their translators more visible.

Jean Boase-Beier

TRANSLATOR'S PREFACE: "ABSURDLY WE HOPE..."

My first attempts at translating Fabio Pusterla's poetry were in 2000, for a literary magazine doing a feature on contemporary Swiss writing. The poet is in fact of mixed Swiss / Italian parentage, teaches Italian literature at the cantonal high school in Lugano, and lives just across the border on the Italian shore of Lake Lugano (Lago di Ceresio) in one of the villages of the Valsolda. I had become acquainted with this area many years before, when I was a teaching assistant in Monza. My French teacher at school had translated Antonio Fogazzaro's *Piccolo mondo antico*, a nineteenth-century novel set in this still rather secluded area. One of life's happy coincidences!

From the beginning, Fabio was generous with his explanations and encouragement and, as a translator himself (of modern French poets, in particular Philippe Jaccottet), well placed to offer assistance. This selection is drawn from six collections which span his poetic career: *Concessione all'inverno* (1985), *Bocksten* (1989), *Le cose senza storia* (1994), *Pietra sangue* (1999), *Folla sommersa* (2004), and *Corpo Stellare* (2011).

The themes are many and varied. In the background is always a strong sense of civilisation under threat, darkness closing in. How does one resist, retain one's humanity, in the dehumanising age in which we live, with its cruelty, wars, misinformation, consumerism, dumbed-down mass entertainment, environmental degradation? Though constantly present, these 'givens' are always treated with restraint. Aware of a spareness and austerity about his poetry – which I would now say was more 'Alpine' than specifically Swiss, perhaps born of the age-old struggle with a harsh natural environment – I recently asked Fabio if he could fairly be described as a Stoic. Amused, I think, he replied that Stoicism, as he understood it, did not allow much room for love or hope, was too passionless or dispassionate.

So here we have a tension of forces in conflict: darkness and light, despair and hope, isolation and human contact, survival against the odds, even though we do not know what shape the future may take. It is evident from many of the poems that Fabio draws great strength from his family and observing his children grow up. He is dedicated to his work as a teacher and has recently published a book about his teaching experience and efforts to pass on the love of reading and literature to the next generation (*Una goccia di splendore. Riflessioni sulla scuola, nonostante tutto*, Casagrande, 2008). He has pondered the experience of parents and grandparents and the importance of collective memory and community. The presence of birds and animals, and the often unforgiving landscape itself, testifies to a love of the natural world.

Then there are those unanticipated "moments of grace": moments when the veil of everyday reality is miraculously lifted and "allegria" (mirth, joy, gladness) "bubbles up... / and flies, even on the darkest evenings, / on tiny, tiny wings" (p. 99).

Although not primarily a literary translator, I have become almost addicted to the task of wresting meaning from a foreign language text and finding a form of words that conveys it in English. With poetry, patience is undoubtedly the best strategy: contemplating a poem and letting it work in the mind until it slowly begins to offer suggestions and yield secrets. Some of these poems are relatively easy of access, others more hermetic. I realise I am in a privileged position, having benefited from Fabio's explanations of the situations and circumstances that inspired some of his more difficult passages. Some notes are included, mainly Fabio's, but also a few of my own to help with interpretation. On the whole though, we thought it best to let the poems speak for themselves and leave scope for the reader's imagination.

Those familiar with Italian writing may recognise some literary references. 'The Eel of the Rhine', for instance, is a response to Eugenio's Montale's poem 'L'anguilla', taking up the word 'sister', with which Montale's poem ends. The migratory eel, a great survivor, is even more our sister as it now has to contend with the pollution of its environment. There are also Dantesque references: to the wood of the suicides (*Inferno* XIII) in 'Bois de la folie'; to Dante's meeting with Guido Guinizelli (*Purgatorio* XXVI) in 'In cammino'.

Fabio Pusterla's poetry has previously been translated into

French, German, Spanish and Serbo-Croat. I hope this selection of poems will bring his poetic voice, with its sensitive combination of concern and restraint, to the attention of the English-speaking world. I would particularly like to thank the Swiss Arts Council and Translation House Looren for enabling me to stay in beautiful surroundings overlooking Lake Zurich while I completed the task.

Simon Knight

INTRODUCTION

To begin with, my credentials for contributing this introduction to the work of an outstanding poet rendered into English for the first time here by a very distinguished translator: principally they are that I am a passionate reader of poetry, both for pleasure and for keeping regular reviewing deadlines; and that I write it; and that I have made staged translations of classic poetic dramas. But then I come to this absorbing task as someone who does not speak and cannot read Italian. An A Level in Latin some while ago, and the more recent acquisition of a smattering of everyday Romanian, may have helped me, a very little. Nevertheless, virtually all of my appreciation of Fabio Pusterla's achievement has depended on Simon Knight's wonderful ability to make his poems accessible, exciting and mysteriously moving as English poems in their own right.

It would be quite possible to take them as such if they were not accompanied by the original texts on the facing pages. But those are a compelling encouragement to the venturesome reader, with or without a knowledge of the language translated, to compare the look of the words (if not the sound) and the structures of the poems. Perhaps they will even be for some, with Simon Knight's scrupulously faithful line-by-line versions (he is aided by the lucidity and compactness of the poems), an incentive to learn it. I hope so. But understanding and appreciating these powerful poems should come first.

Fabio Pusterla's poetry is firmly set in a characteristic modern landscape with which most readers will be familiar, but of which they need regular reminders in case they gradually acquiesce in what has happened to it, and continues to happen: ignorant neglect or disrespect, casual pollution, outright and shameless destruction. Here, from the first poem onwards, is the erosion of soil and stone which can erase mountains, "the forests felled" (p. 25), the dodo extinguished, the tourist bay rendered synonymous with Charon's Styx on account of oil slicks, the tar staining the abandoned suitcase (a metaphor for civility?), the out-of-town supermarket serving as most people's only meeting-place. The literal danger to all life on the planet in what now threatens to become an unstoppable deterioration is something of which we are now much better aware than in the past, except for those in cynical (and profitable?) denial that any of this is real. Fabio Pusterla realises the need to reiterate the case against the polluters. So do environmental campaigners, who will provide the evidence, the statistics and the prophetic warnings. But the poet's role is to uncover and highlight the frightening or poignant details, actual or imagined, which stand for and symbolise the entire process; and that Pusterla fulfils admirably.

It would be difficult to read him if he was solely a writer emphasising (in the poem titled 'Parentheses' p. 23) "the loss of certainties and affirmations", with mere "parentheses, incidentals and interjections" providing our only foundation for the future. Over half a century ago the critic François Duchêne spoke of the modern (possibly modernist?) atmosphere of cultural despair in which "Eliot, Rilke, Valéry unveiled themselves as monuments of diffidence". Now, those great figures seem more like pillars supporting by example everything of worth in cultural activity. Pusterla can be a 'diffident' writer; but there is an implicit affirmation of the same values in the combination of strength and imaginative delicacy with which he approaches his subjects. It would be going too far to believe that the ending of 'The Eel of the Rhine' (p. 27) offers hope, but at least "The instinct to swim, because the sea / is a distant fragrance, the hint / of a dream interrupted just before daybreak" affirms something: "an idea of life [to be extracted] / from the factual evidence, a final challenge [to be derived] from anxiety, Utopia / [to be constructed] from our common fear" (my own square brackets).

The passages just quoted are from Pusterla's two earliest books. With the third, *Things With No Past* (1994), the theme of family and childhood becomes important and provides an undertone of gentleness: children are affectionately observed sleeping, playing, writing in a notebook. Fear is still there in the poem titled 'Buried in the Garden' (p. 29), as a "power we shall have to break"; but an unmistakeable Wordsworthian note is sounded as he watches his child exploring the surroundings:

> ... You are in your pre-history
> of silences and cries,
> and burning discoveries: sun, fire,
> train whistles, tunnels.
> Language will come later,
> things will have names and maybe less
> vividness, less splendour. And memory
> will build you coralline barriers, stars fixed
> in time. But for now there's no distance,
> no gap.

More often, though, he is alarmed for his children's sake at what he sees. In 'Landscape' (p. 37) he is surveying a whole panorama of desolation in one small corner:

> Then the hen-house. Things with no past.
> Or outside. A wheelbarrow
> with no wheel. A well. A rusted bucket
> with no bottom. The name of an idiot:
> Luigino. Feathers in the netting, chickens'.
> Holes in the netting. Broken mesh.
> What you do not call cruelty.

Does the final line sum up the effect of various minor acts of neglect? Nothing cruel has been perpetrated, mere indifference has produced this dismaying prospect. In 'Breaking Surface' (p. 47), one of his most enigmatic and haunting poems at this stage, a curious fantasy of birds improbably nesting under the sea and presumably emerging – "we must greet them kindly, acknowledge them, / softly brush away the darkness from their shivering, / gently persuade them to stay" – provides a temporary relief. But in 'Continente' (p. 53), which the Notes reveal to be "the name of a vast new shopping complex in Portugal", he experiences a shocked and disgusted amazement at this pinnacle of commercial achievement:

> Tons of rice and pasta. Aisles
> of tinned food: sardines, palm hearts.
> Cloves by the billion.
> Nine years of our lives, they say,

are spent queuing in traffic:
where do all the thoughts go,
it would be nice to know, even
recycle them.

From this point onwards, the poems in this selection show an appreciably wider range and a hugely increased confidence, and begin to acquire something very like major status. In the poem with that title (p. 55), the Two Adversaries are "gutted matter / and bright limpid light." The sight of a shrew emerging from the dark of its burrow in an Alpine midwinter suggests to the poet crucial qualities of daring and endurance. The creature appears to survive on "particles of watery light", and Pusterla's vision of his surroundings is suddenly transformed. As the mist parts –

there, where chance directs the gaze,
appears, in clarity, a swathe of mountain, but detached
from earth, as if in flight: immense eagle
of black rock and snow, talon and wing.

Matter is no longer simply eroded, or gutted. It is threatened, certainly, as some poems which follow still imply: see 'Drainage Canal', 'Two Herons' or 'Deposition'. But it remains capable of defiant grandeur, and there is always hope in the survival of other creatures than the shrew: a blackbird, a wild goat (leaving a gift of "tiny brown / droppings, and on the air a scent of wilderness", p. 75) and a "displaced swarm" (p. 87) of wasps.

My second and third examples are from a substantial last section of more recent poems. In 'April 2006. Postcards of Italy' (p. 99) Pusterla celebrates, with a fine blend of protest and pity with irony and doubt, the narrow defeat of the earlier Berlusconi government by the votes of Italian workers in exile – to whom it had granted the suffrage for the first time. They have left Italy for a destiny of

...dams, tunnels, mines, railroads,
later motorways, factories,

> but still the same surrender, the same effort
> of shoulders and bowed heads...

They have learned to do without a country the poet can only see as polluted and compromised, "the lemon tree faded, withered, / lemon stolen". Still, they have gratifyingly returned with their votes "a hint of civic decency, the emigrants' revenge." This even though Pusterla is reflecting on their achievement during a snarl-up on a motorway which "seethes with irritation: people phoning or smoking, / taking pictures of an unfamiliar landscape". That represents everything he resents and despises, and the poem ends on a note of bewildered despair with the image of a well-to-do, indifferent stranger who bears

> ...the air of
> a winner, who knows he is always a winner:
> but what in fact has he won?
>
> He is what he is, I maybe me, no one is us.

He seems there to have become simultaneously a discerning social poet and one who has relinquished any hope that collective action (by "us") to counter the infamies of the age.

But the final poem here, 'Stories of the Armadillo' (p. 113), concludes the selection in a slightly more sanguine style – of resistance and persistence. What began as a joke has changed into a delightful extended satire ranging over most of his themes. Like the shrew in 'The Two Adversaries', the Armadillo, when necessary, lives underground, digging "long burrows, dark damp places in which to await / better days, rain, times when hope / is not completely impossible...". Moving on, it is guided by "the idea / of armadillo", symbolising a kind of obstinate, dogged rebellion against the terrain through which it travels, far too experienced ever to panic or lose courage. We are invited to suspect all this is serious allegory, and we surely do. Tickle the Armadillo and he laughs, causing unease in those who hear him. He is

> ...thinking
> of all this hatred, violence, greed,

and everything ultimately ridiculous, lost
in the vacuity of the ages....

Fabio Pusterla is seeing this awkward, illogical, somewhat feared animal (an American state has forbidden anybody to own one) as what a poet might aspire to resemble. His Notes end: "Run, armadillo, run!"
Maybe me?

Alan Brownjohn

DAYS FULL OF CAVES AND TIGERS
GIORNI PIENI DI CAVERNE E DI TIGRI

da
CONCESSIONE ALL'INVERNO
(1985)

LE PARENTESI

L'erosione
cancellerà le Alpi, prima scavando valli,
poi ripidi burroni, vuoti insanabili
che preludono al crollo, gorghi. Lo scricchiolio
sarà il segnale di fuga: questo il verdetto.
Rimarranno le pozze, i montaruzzi casuali,
le pause di riposo, i sassi rotolanti,
le caverne e le piane paludose.
Nel Mondo Nuovo rimarranno, cadute
principali e alberi sintattici, sperse
certezze e affermazioni,
le parentesi, gli incisi e le interiezioni:
le palafitte del domani.

PARADISO, CAPRINO, CAVALLINO

Io credo che un vecchio
da qualche parte immobile sul quai
(scura ombra antistante l'acqua marcia)
in bilico sul margine, dove straborda
l'onda al passaggio di parodie di navi,

un marinaio d'acqua dolce, cupo
turistico Caronte lungo il golfo,
guardi la sera il lago.
Da impronunciabili presagi apprende
che di sotto (egli sa) usciranno.

from
CONCESSION TO WINTER
(1985)

PARENTHESES

Erosion
will erase the Alps, first scoring valleys,
then deep ravines, bottomless pits
foreshadowing the collapse, chasms. A groaning
will be the signal for flight: this the verdict.
Left will be pools, chance mounds,
pauses for rest, erratic boulders,
caves and marshy plains.
In the New World, after the fall
of syntax trees and main clauses, the loss
of certainties and affirmations, left will be
parentheses, incidentals and interjections:
the pile-works of tomorrow.

PARADISO, CAPRINO, CAVALLINO

I believe an old man
somewhere motionless on the embankment
(dark shadow facing the stagnant water)
hovering on the edge, where the swell
overlaps as parodies of ships pass by,

a fresh-water sailor, surly
Charon taking trippers round the bay,
watches the lake at evening.
From unspeakable portents he learns
that from below (he knows) they will emerge.

(I pochi morti annegati non vengono
di solito tratti in superficie:
correnti ignote e mobili fondali, lucci,
alghe incolori arrestano
il transito dei pallidi).

Verranno
una notte inattesa e prenderanno
possesso della città: nerastri, untuosi,
le algose chiome sciogliendo,
a sconvolgere verranno, per tingere,
infine, di catrame
i rami, e benzinose essenze.

IL DRONTE

E se le sprofondanti immensità temevi
sopra o sotto, i marosi o il vento,
riparo le rocce ancora erano, alla novità ventosa,
allo spruzzo, all'orrore del fondo.
Era un regno di basalto, a precipizio
su raggrumate colate di lava, su smangiati coralli.
Ma poi: un luccichio di sestanti, cannocchiali.
Abbattute le foreste piantarono canne da zucchero.
E tu inerte zampettante
prigioniero dell'isola, schiacciato
fra due azzurri diversi, di inesausta durezza.
E muri ciechi, di vele spiegate su caracche, e bandiere,
fiocchi, pappafichi, tonfi d'ancora. E ghigni
di topi, pipisterelli, camaleonti e gechi.

(The few drownees are not usually
carried to the surface:
unknown currents and shifting shoals, pike,
colourless algae impede
the progress of the pallid ones).

They will come
one night unexpected and take
possession of the town: blackish, slimy,
weedy locks dishevelled,
to wreak havoc they will come, to stain,
at any rate, the branches
with tar and oily substances.

THE DODO

And if you feared the giddying immensity
above or below, breeze or breaker,
the rocks were still your refuge from what the wind might bring,
the spray, the horror of the deep.
Yours was a kingdom of basalt, high above
clotted lava flows, rolled and eroded coral.
But then: the glint of sextant and spyglass.
The forests felled, they planted sugarcane.
And you, indolent plodder,
prisoner of the island, trapped
between blue and blue, each of unyielding hardness.
And blind walls, of canvas spread on carracks, and flags,
staysails, top-gallants, the splash of anchors. And the jeers
of rats, bats, chameleons and geckos.

da
BOCKSTEN
(1989)

L'ANGUILLA DEL RENO

Adesso sì, sorella, e più di prima,
se guizzi disperata tra scoli d'atrazina
e getti d'olio vischioso;
o se colpisci di coda, estenuata,
la carezza dell'onda di fosfati che s'annera
sulla ghiaia della riva
(la riva, il greto,
il melmoso sabbione
frugati dalle torce delle squadre,
sfrecciano via elicotteri, lampeggiano
bluastre le sirene bitonali),
se adesso persino il Baltico è perduto,
circoscritto il viaggio
nell'armilla d'incendi e d'esplosioni,
e ti rituffi ai relitti, ai tesori del fondo,
chiglie corrose e catene d'ancoraggio,
a precipizio per correnti verticali, masse d'acqua
più fredde, dove scopri il tuo brivido,
un istinto di nuoto, perché il mare
è un profumo lontanissimo, il sospetto
di un sogno interrotto poco prima dell'alba,
quanto basta alla pinna e al tuo testardo
palpito delle branchie, per strappare
un attimo all'asfissia, un'idea di vita
all'evidenza dei fatti, l'ultima sfida all'ansia, un'utopia
alla paura di tutti.

from
BOCKSTEN
(1989)

THE EEL OF THE RHINE

Now sister indeed, and more than ever,
as you wriggle desperate through spills of atrazine
and slicks of viscous oil;
or, exhausted, beat your tail against
the caressing wave of phosphates blackening
the gravel on the shore
(the shore, the strand,
the sludgy shingle
probed by the torches of the rescue teams,
helicopters dart away, two-tone
sirens flash their bluish lights),
as now even the Baltic is doomed,
your journey circumscribed
by a steel ring of fires and explosions,
and you dive back down to sunken treasures, the wreckage of
rusted hulls and anchor chains,
down through vertical currents, masses of
colder water, where you find a quiver of life,
the instinct to swim, because the sea
is a distant fragrance, the hint
of a dream interrupted just before daybreak,
enough for your fins and stubbornly
palpitating gills to wrest a moment
from asphyxiation, an idea of life
from the factual evidence, a final challenge from anxiety, utopia
from our common fear.

da
LE COSE SENZA STORIA
(1994)

SONNO DI CLAUDIA E NINA

Dicevi che di giorno
il buio sta negli armadi,
o dietro i monti,
e viene fuori solo verso sera,
quando si può dormire
e aver paura.
Però stanotte è insonnia, luna piena,
e dietro ogni fessura pulsa l'aria
magnetica, indovino
quasi ogni piega dei boschi.
Così conto i respiri
a voi, corpi qui accanto: un'onda lunga
che sale piano e scende, che ritorna,
e sotto abissi, danza di murene.

SOTTO IL GIARDINO

1

Dove porta questa strada che nessuno più imbocca,
strada appena intuibile, sentiero
d'erbacce?
Qui gente rotolava sulla pancia, sghignazzando,
e c'erano molte grida, anche di dolore.

from
THINGS WITH NO PAST
(1994)

CLAUDIA AND NINA SLEEPING

You used to say that by day
the darkness stays in the wardrobes
or behind the mountains,
and comes out only at dusk
when we can sleep
and be afraid.
But tonight insomnia, full moon,
and through every crack pulsates
the magnetic air, I sense
almost every nook of the woods.
So I count the breaths
of your bodies here beside me: a long wave
which slowly rises, falls, withdraws,
and deep down dance the conger eels.

BURIED IN THE GARDEN

1

Where leads this road that no one now takes,
barely discernible, weed-grown
pathway?
Here people rolled on their bellies, with coarse mocking laughter,
and there was much shouting, and cries of pain.

(Esiste, esiste anche senza di noi,
la possibilità di un cammino.
Bisognerà appiattarsi nell'erba, scordare qualcosa,
e te, maledetta paura,
dovremo proprio sconfiggerti).

2
a Matteo

C'era come un pudore a confessarci
l'abitudine all'intrico delle edere,
gli spinosi macchioni di robinie, e quei sentieri
cercati a lungo, scoperti e ancora perduti
nell'ignoranza dei sottoboschi.
Non se ne parla, ci si va, pensavi,
insegnandomi una città immaginaria
che costruivi in un paese senza sole:
in silenzio, anche perché le parole
erano contate, non bisognava sprecarle.

7

Non abbiamo nient'altro:
un'allegria di gesti, di sorrisi,
un corpo che si muove fra quattro muri nudi.
È un temporale d'agosto il suono breve
sulle ringhiere a picco verso il lago,
il vortice più scuro che rinfresca,
un tuffo di poiana. Fuori è notte.

8

Gli odori forti, la menta e il limoncino,
sembrano darti fastidio. I sassi, i rapanelli,

(It is possible, even without us,
to walk this way.
One must flatten oneself in the grass, let something go,
and as for you, cursed fear,
your power we shall have to break).

2
for Matteo

There was a kind of shyness to confess
our familiarity with the tangled ivy,
the thickets of spiny acacia, and those pathways
long sought, found and lost again
in our ignorance of the underwood.
Action, not words, you thought,
introducing me to an imaginary city
you were building in a sunless land:
in silence, and because words were numbered,
better not waste them.

7

We have nothing else:
the happiness of smiles and gestures,
a body moving among four bare walls.
The tip-tapping on the guard rails high above the lake
announces an August storm,
a dark refreshing downdraught,
the dive of a buzzard. Outside it is night.

8

Strong smells, of mint and verbena,
you seem to find off-putting. Stones, radishes,

gli oggetti dimenticati nel giardino
ti attirano allo scavo, alla scoperta: gocce d'acqua
sui tubi, zappe rotte,
il buio del sottoscala, ragnatele. Una moneta
salta fuori dell'orto, un re coi baffi
da centesimi cinque, e vuoi mangiarlo.
Chi l'ha perso vangava nel primo novecento:
patate, forse (era tempo di guerra);
e così sulla terra dei morti
crescono i fagiolini rampicanti.

9

Non ricorderai niente.
Il cane Igor, cremina per il sole,
e quando ti diverti a fare il vento
e soffi e ridi. Sei nella tua preistoria
di silenzi e di gridi,
di brucianti scoperte: sole, fuoco,
e sirene di treni, gallerie.
Dopo verrà la lingua,
le cose avranno nomi e forse meno
intensità, meno splendore. E la memoria
ti costruirà barriere coralline, stelle fisse
nel tempo. Ma adesso non c'è distanza,
non c'è vuoto.

10

La sera, foglie secche nelle tasche,
ghiande di quercia, certi sassi colorati.
Tu li raccogli, e me li dai: frantumi
minuscoli del giorno, o tracce del pensiero. Qui
è passato un cane, il lupo forse non c'è,
adesso voglio una foglia grandissima, e dopo? dopo no.

objects abandoned in the garden
tempt you to dig and explore: water dripping
from pipes, broken hoes,
the darkness under the stair, cobwebs. A coin
resurrected from the vegetable patch, five-cent
bewhiskered king, you put to your mouth.
Lost in the early nineteen hundreds
by someone digging, potatoes maybe (it was wartime);
and thus on the land of the dead
spring forth runner beans.

9

You will remember nothing.
The dog Igor, sun cream,
and the fun of imitating the wind,
blowing and laughing. You are in your pre-history
of silences and cries,
and burning discoveries: sun, fire,
train whistles, tunnels.
Language will come later,
things will have names and maybe less
vividness, less splendour. And memory
will build you coralline barriers, stars fixed
in time. But for now there's no distance,
no gap.

10

Evening, pockets full of dry leaves,
acorns, coloured stones
you collect and give me: tiny
fragments of the day, or scraps of thought.
A dog's been here; perhaps the wolf's away,
now I want a giant leaf, and then? Then nothing.

Proprio come i capelli di tua madre: dappertutto
quasi invisibili, più veloci di me.

11

Non vermicelli: lettere,
framenti d'alfabeto
simili a dei girini in uno stagno
o ai rospi canterini d'Argentan.
Così polvere, giorni,
l'estate intera si è dissolta in brodo,
e ora è minestra, inverno,
c'è fumo nel cucchiaio, brina sui vetri.
Cerca le vocali più dolci, i suoni caldi,
luci e parole in crescita.

TRE FRAMMENTI DELLA DISDETTA

a mia madre

I

Certe case non sono solo case:
relitti affioranti, su scogliere
dove il vento è più implacabile, forte,
e il grido di dolore si confonde
col rumore del mare.
Lo squalo che le sfiora con la pinna
dorsale, disattento,
nemmeno se ne accorge. Ma ci sono.

Just like your mother's hair: everywhere,
almost invisible, too quick for me.

11

Not vermicelli: letters,
alphabetic fragments,
like tadpoles in a pond
or the singing toads of Argentan.
So dust, days,
the whole of summer has reduced to broth,
and become a soup, winter,
there's steam in the spoon, frost on the windows.
Pick the softest vowels, warm sounds,
lights and words growing stronger.

NOTICE TO QUIT: THREE FRAGMENTS

for my mother

I

Some houses are not just houses:
emergent wrecks, on reefs
where the wind blows more implacable, strong,
and the cry of pain mingles
with the roar of the ocean.
The shark that grazes them,
careless, with its dorsal fin,
does not even notice. But they are there.

II

"Nel nostro paese
il sole si alza verso Monte Olimpino
e va giù dalle parti di Seseglio. A mezzogiorno
si trova Pedrinate e il bosco Penz, ricco di funghi
e roveti. Come riferimento
prendiamo la Casa dei Ladri".

III

Vieni,
dobbiamo andare.
Tanto qui
non c'è più nulla da fare.

PAESAGGIO

Qui piove per giorni interi, talvolta per mesi.
I sassi sono neri d'acquate,
i sentieri pesanti.

*

Sul bordo delle rogge:
girini, latte scure. Una valigia
incatramata.

*

II

"In our village
the sun rises by Mount Olimpino
and goes down towards Seseglio. To the south
are Pedrinate and Penz Wood, rich in mushroom
and bramble. Our landmark
is the House of Thieves".

III

Come,
it is time to go.
Anyway, here
there is no more to be done.

LANDSCAPE

Here it rains for days on end, sometimes for months,
The rocks are streaked black with water,
the paths heavy going.

*

On the edge of the ditches:
tadpoles, rusted cans. A tar-stained
suitcase.

*

Un filo d'olio cola
sulla ghiaia. Sopra, cemento.
Se gratti la terra: detriti,
mattoni scagliati, denti di coniglio.

*

Si possono pensare rumori umani,
passi, palle da tennis. Voci eventuali.
Ogni frantume è ammesso purché inutile.

*

Siccome questo è il vuoto c'è posto per tutto,
e quel poco che c'è, è come non ci fosse.
Anche i binari sono perfettamente inerti,
le lucertole immobili, i vagoni
dimenticati.

*

E poi il pollaio. Le cose senza storia.
O fuori. Una carriola
che non ha ruote. Un pozzo. Un secchio marcio
privo di fondo. Il nome di uno scemo:
Luigino. Piume dentro la rete, di gallina.
Buchi dentro la rete. Trame rotte.
Quello che non chiamate crudeltà.

*

Io sono questo: niente.
Voglio quello che sono, fortemente.
E le parole: nessuno adesso me le ruberà.

A dribble of oil runs
on the gravel. Above, cement.
Scratch the ground: refuse,
crumbling bricks, rabbits' teeth.

*

One can imagine the sounds of human presence,
footsteps, tennis balls. Voices even.
Every fragment permitted provided it serves no purpose.

*

This being emptiness there's room for everything,
and what little there is, it's as if it wasn't there.
Even the railway tracks are perfectly inert,
the lizards motionless, the wagons
abandoned.

*

Then the hen-house. Things with no past.
Or outside. A wheelbarrow
with no wheel. A well. A rusted bucket
with no bottom. The name of an idiot:
Luigino. Feathers in the netting, chickens'.
Holes in the netting. Broken mesh.
What you do not call cruelty.

*

I am this: nothing,
I want what I am, strongly.
And my words: no one will now steal them from me.

NEVICARE (O SCRIVERE D'INVERNO)

Sorprendere in silenzio la città addormentata
portando la formula del freddo
e il cielo muto,
lambire fili tesi, rami secchi,
posarsi, sfarsi, diluirsi
senza rumore o vento,
scendere bianca inattesa,
senza peso
ricoprire
la strada, la panca, la casa.

I CROCUS DI EVOLÈNE

a Guenda

Ho spazzolato con cura le mie scarpe infangate,
ho cucito un bottone ai pantaloni. Poi, nel parco,
ho osservato i primi fiori di magnolia, e il becco giallo
di un merlo. Ai piedi delle montagne
piccoli fiori viola sbucano dalla neve,
accennano la strada a chi si è perso.

L'ANNEGATA

È un'acqua bassa,
che guadano i cinghiali
nottetempo, lasciando sulle rive
tracce disordinate.
Ma come poteva saperlo,
lei, che veniva da così lontano?

SNOWING (OR WRITING IN WINTER)

Silently surprising the sleeping city
bearing the formula of cold
and a mute sky,
brushing taught wires, sapless
branches,
settling, melting, dissolving
without sound or wind,
falling white and unexpected,
weightless
covering
road, bench and house.

CROCUSES AT EVOLÈNE

for Guenda

Carefully I brushed my muddy shoes,
sewed a button on my trousers; then, in the park,
observed the first magnolia flowers, and the yellow beak
of a blackbird. At the foot of the mountains
little purple flowers are piercing the snow,
pointing the way to those who are lost.

THE DROWNED WOMAN

The water there is shallow;
the wild boar ford it
at night, leaving their unruly tracks
on the banks.
But how was she to know,
coming from so far away?

Sarà stata una pozza imprevedibile,
la fatica, un sasso viscido o quella paura
che può cogliere alla fine di un viaggio:
e forse aveva già capito di non avere speranza.

CRESPI D'ADDA

Lungo i due lati del viale d'accesso
in doppia fila
si dispongano le tombe dei bambini:
piccole pietre uguali.
Il termine "bambino"
vuole indicare chi non ha raggiunto
l'età idonea al lavoro

*

Si evitino
le formule patetiche.
Il grande edificio grigio sullo sfondo
suggerisce compostezza
e abnegazione.

*

Di fronte al cimitero
la natura ha disposto il suo omaggio:
grano e papaveri.
Ciò sia di sprone a tutti
affinché l'ordine regni in ogni orto.

*

It must have been a sudden deep spot,
tiredness, a slippery rock, or the fear
that can grip one at the end of a journey:
and maybe she already knew her case was hopeless.

CRESPI D'ADDA

Let the graves of the children
be arranged in two rows
on either side of the avenue:
small stones all the same.
The term 'child'
means one who has not reached
working age.

*

Let us avoid
sentimentality.
The great grey monument in the background
bespeaks dignity
and self-denial.

*

Opposite the cemetery
nature has arranged its tribute:
corn and poppies.
Let it be a spur to all,
that order reign in every garden.

*

La geometria perfetta delle strade
non è senza rapporto
col senso di dovere: ricordàtelo.
Un giorno
tutto sarà così.

*

Se qualcuno
volesse per avventura andare altrove,
faccia pure.
Sappia però di non avere alternative.

PAESAGGIO CON MOIRA CHE SCRIVE

All'alba Moira scrive su un quaderno
nel corridoio del treno, accovacciata. Un uomo grasso
si sbuccia una banana, su una fabbrica
tramonta il primo sole, e poi è la pioggia
che annuncia la Germania : pioggia fine.

Batte sui vetri adesso
un giorno come gli altri, di lavoro, e il treno in corsa
è il suo vessillo scuro, una sirena
metallica che assembla
frammenti di pianura, case e destini
uguali. È l'alba,
un giorno esausto di mezza stagione.

The perfect geometry of the streets
is not unrelated
to a sense of duty: bear it in mind.
One day
everything will be like this.

*

If anyone
should perchance want to go elsewhere,
he is free to do so.
But be aware: there is no alternative.

LANDSCAPE WITH MOIRA WRITING

At dawn Moira writes in a notebook
in the train corridor, hunched over. A fat man
peels a banana, the early sun
fades on a factory, and it is rain,
a fine drizzle, that heralds Germany.

On the windows now presses
a day like any other, a work day, and the speeding train
is its dark banner, a metallic
siren that gathers
fragments of the plain, houses and common
destinies. Dawn,
on a flat in-between-season day.

IL MERLO

Se fischia
verso il chiaro, e il giorno è solo
una fessura grigia dentro il freddo,
nessuno può sentirlo: nel garage
è ancora buio, sporadici
sussulti di lamiera. Bandiere azzurre immobili.
Sul ghiaccio
passa un soffio di vento, quasi un brivido,
un cavo d'acciaio sbatte. E se col becco
fruga nel nero delle penne o cerca
la briciola fra i sassi, il filo verde
che stenta nella crepa,
tu guardalo più attento: ecco, un motore
tossisce dietro l'angolo,
stanchezze puntuali si rinzelano. Ma il merlo
saltella, alza la testa,
prende il volo.

LE TERRE EMERSE

Là, dove nidificheranno molti uccelli.

Insisti nello scrutare a lungo il mare
diffidando del tuo sguardo disabile.

No, niente di maestoso, per fortuna.
Piuttosto una nuova calma, una diversa
geometria della spuma.

THE BLACKBIRD

If it whistles
towards the dawning, and the day is only
a grey cleft in the coldness,
no one can hear it: in the garage
it is still dark, sporadic
groanings of corrugated iron. Blue flags motionless.
Over the ice
comes a breath of wind, almost a shiver,
a steel cable slaps. And if with its beak
it probes its black feathers or searches for
a crumb among the stones, a thread of greenery
surviving in a crack,
watch more closely: there, an engine
coughs just round the corner,
the weary responding punctual to duty. But the blackbird
hops, lifts its head,
takes wing.

BREAKING SURFACE

There, where many birds will nest.

You persist in scrutinising the ocean
distrusting your feeble eye.

No, nothing majestic, fortunately.
Just a renewed calm, a different
configuration of the foam.

Si vorrebbe raggiungerle
proprio nei giorni peggiori, quando le onde
sembrano ghiaccio azzurro, il cielo pesa
più grigio, e unico scampo
rimane l'improbabile.

Se ci sono,
se brillano sotto il pelo
dell'acqua, inconosciute
eppure attese, fuori vista,
saranno lastre verdi di sasso,
lievemente inclinate.

L'emersione
si addebita alle forze
e alle frizioni che sconvolgono il fondo,
a una orrenda pressione in assenza
di ogni altra possibilità.
Un lunghissimo periodo di mestizia
si può considerare inevitabile.

Avranno freddo anche loro, intirizzite,
e forse pioverà, ci sarà il vento.
Dovremo accoglierle bene, riconoscerle,
scostare adagio il buio dai loro brividi,
convincerle dolcemente a rimanere.
La geografia e tutte le coordinate
cambieranno da sole, senza fretta;
ci vorrà un po' di tempo per capire.

E poi non devi illuderti: vedremo
al massimo l'inizio,
la timida colonia dei molluschi, un po' di bava

One would like to reach them
on the very worst days, when the waves
look like blue ice, the sky weighs
greyer, and the improbable
still provides the only exit.

If they are there,
if they glisten under the water's
surface, unknown
yet awaited, out of sight,
they must be green slabs of rock,
tilted slightly.

Their emergence
is due to forces
and frictions convulsing the seabed,
horrendous pressure in the absence
of any other possibility.
A very long period of destitution
may be considered inevitable.

They, too, will be cold, benumbed,
and maybe it will rain, the wind will blow.
We must greet them kindly, acknowledge them,
softly brush away the darkness from their shivering,
gently persuade them to stay.
Geography and all the co-ordinates
will take care of themselves, no hurry;
it will take a while to understand.

And then, don't fool yourself: we shall see
at most a beginning,
a timid colony of molluscs, a dribble

d'alga bagnata nelle scanalature,
la sosta di un gabbiano, un grido roco
che sembra senza senso o troppo fragile,
eppure si propaga, si moltiplica.
I fiori, l'erba e le altre cose bellissime
verranno forse dopo. Ma ci basta.

VATEL

> *il courut un cerf au clair de la lune; les lanternes firent*
> *des merveilles*
> Mme. de Sévigné

Ho fatto il mio dovere
cipolla dopo cipolla: questo lo sai.
Ti ho servito
come sapevo. Ma adesso,
nella notte dei tuoi fuochi di vittoria,
tra queste signorine per bene
che domani scriveranno di me alle loro amiche
piene d'orrore, e questi cigni
candidi sopra il lago
artificiale, la bambagia dei giorni
non ha onore né gloria,
motivo d'allegria.
Me ne vado, signore. A te l'ebbrezza
di un dolce mai provato, le figure
di mille sughi d'arrosto.
Con me prenderò l'alba.
Il sale e il freddo.

of wet seaweed in the cracks,
a seagull alighting, a raucous cry
which seems senseless or too fragile,
and yet spreads and multiplies.
Flowers, grass and other things of beauty
may come later. But we shall rest content.

VATEL

> *il courut un cerf au clair de la lune; les lanternes firent*
> *des merveilles*
> Mme. de Sévigné

I have done my duty
onion by onion: this you know.
I have served you
as best I could. But now,
on the night of your triumphal fireworks,
among these well-bred young ladies
who tomorrow will write horrified of me
to their friends, and these immaculate swans
on the artificial lake,
the cossetting of the days
brings neither honour nor glory,
no cause for gladness.
Farewell, my Lord. I leave you the frisson
of an untried dessert, recipes
for a thousand sauces.
With me I take the dawn.
The salt and the cold.

CONTINENTE

Vorrebbe sapere cosa capita,
quello che si prepara.
Cosa vedono, di giorno,
quelli che vengono qui: ottocentomila
ogni mese, pare; quasi due milioni
di occhi in transito,
di mani che afferrano.
Come vedono. Come cambiano, per dire,
l'amore o il dolore, l'insonnia.
Quintali di riso e pasta. Corridoi
di scatolame; sardine, cuori di palma.
Chiodi di garofano: miliardi.
Nove anni di vita, dicono,
passati in coda nel traffico:
dove vanno i pensieri,
sarebbe bello saperlo, riciclarli,
magari. Poi: è vero che questo
è il nuovo concetto di "luogo d'incontro"?
Che la clessidra idraulica dell'ingegner Gitton
è la più grande del mondo?
Che è stata messa qui
non senza un motivo simbolico?

CONTINENTE

He would like to know what's going on,
what's cooking.
What they see, in the daytime,
the people who come here: eight hundred thousand of them
each month, apparently; almost two million
eyes in transit,
two million grasping hands.
How they see things. How they deal with, say,
love or pain, insomnia.
Tons of rice and pasta. Aisles
of tinned food: sardines, palm hearts.
Cloves by the billion.
Nine years of our lives, they say,
are spent queuing in traffic:
where do all the thoughts go,
it would be nice to know, even
recycle them. And is it true that this
is the new concept of a "meeting place"?
That engineer Gitton's water clock
is the largest in the world?
That it was put here
not without symbolic intent?

da
PIETRA SANGUE
(1999)

I DUE AVVERSARI

Betulla impietrita dal gelo, catasta nera
di legna gravata di neve e dentro il cielo
come una strozzatura, vento o ghiaccio. C'è un silenzio
totale, dunque, un ciclo
che nessuna pietà può rompere o descrivere, un inverno
cieco, che non ammette primavera?
Freddo che fende i tronchi, apre le vene
dei campi e li uccide e li guarda morire
e li cancella?

Ma il toporagno, due metri più in là:
cosa fa il toporagno? Saltella,
incide con le sue deboli unghiette la neve,
si ferma brusco e annusa. Cosa annusa?
Poi arriva il sole e va via: chiazze di luce,
gocce di luce ovunque. Particelle
di luce inumidita: il toporagno
si nutre forse di simili sostanze, sopravvive
nell'ombra del suo buco.

E sono qui ambedue: fibra sventrata
e luce chiara e tersa. Due avversari
che non si parlano mai. Dove guardare, ti chiedi,
di quale occhio fidarsi, a chi concedersi.
Se la nebbia si apre, per un attimo,
se il vento delle altezze alza il sipario in un turbine,
proprio là dove il caso indirizza lo sguardo,
appare, chiaro, un lembo di montagna, ma staccata
da terra, quasi in volo: aquila immensa
di roccia nera e neve, artiglio ed ala.

from
**PIETRA SANGUE
(1999)**

THE TWO ADVERSARIES

Birch tree frozen to stone, black stack
of wood laden with snow and in the sky
wind or ice choking off life. Total
silence, then, a cycle
that no mercy can break or describe, blind
winter that will not hear of spring?
Frost that cleaves tree trunks, opens the veins
of the fields, breaks down the clods
and watches them die?

But look, six feet away, a shrew!
What can a shrew be doing? It scurries,
scratches at the snow with feeble claws,
suddenly stops, sniffing. What is there to sniff?
Then the sun comes out and it disappears:
splashes of light, droplets of light everywhere.
Particles of watery light:
maybe the shrew
feeds on such elements, surviving
in the dark of its burrow.

And both are here: gutted matter
and bright limpid light. Adversaries
who never parley. Which way to look, you wonder,
which eye believe, which party yield to.
Should the mist part, for a moment,
should a gust of icy wind from on high raise the curtain,
there, where chance directs the gaze,
appears, in clarity, a swathe of mountain, but detached
from earth, as if in flight: immense eagle
of black rock and snow, talon and wing.

ROGGIA

Passo di qui, tornando da un lungo viaggio,
come in un cimitero di memorie.
La pozzanghera c'è sempre, anche d'estate,
il fango, la sterrata, i ciuffi d'erba
e d'ortica non cambiano mai. Sassi e sterpaglie
spariranno anche loro, soffocati da una morsa
più forte, di cemento, un giorno o l'altro,
e forse prima dei nostri ricordi;
ma per adesso ci sono, ed è il paesaggio
desolato che ho scelto per te. L'ultima casa
aperta al vento e alla luce, una pianura
quasi sempre deserta, non amena,
che percorre lentissima
una roggia. Io fumo, sto sul ponte,
e getto anche per te una sigaretta
nell'acqua scura. È un rito
senza senso, meno ancora che un rito:
un'abitudine. Già con mio padre, a volte, sotto i fiori;
e mi domando cosa avrà pensato mia madre
di quel tabacco tombale: spettri, vandali?
O forse ha indovinato e non ne parla
per pudore. Full flavor blend, comunque, una miscela
mediocre, piuttosto grezza, maryland: la sigaretta
rossa dei muratori, o così dicono. Anche il nome
riporta a sogni lisi e fuori corso: Parisienne,
ragazze che sgambettano su un palco al Moulin Rouge,
le luci di Pigalle, la naftalina di un secolo, BB.
O Jeanne Moreau, col suo volto
vastissimo e profondo: le sarebbe piaciuto
questo tabacco. Oggi però inattesi
dall'argine sono spuntati cinque germani
spaventandomi quasi. Sono scesi in acqua regali,
risalendo la poca corrente della roggia, e uno di loro
si è voltato un istante.

DRAINAGE CANAL

I come this way, back from a long journey,
as if in a graveyard of memories.
The puddle is still here, even in summer;
the mud, the cart track, the clumps of grass
and nettles never change. Stones and brushwood, too,
will disappear, crushed in a more constrictive vice
of cement, one day or another,
and maybe even sooner than our memories;
but for now they exist, and this is the desolate
landscape I have chosen for you. The last house
open to wind and sunlight, a flat expanse
almost always deserted, unprepossessing,
through which a sluggish canal
pursues its course. I stand on the bridge and smoke
and throw a cigarette into the dark water
for you, too. A senseless rite,
not even a rite: a habit.
Just as I did with my father, sometimes, under the flowers;
and I wonder what my mother must have thought
of that sepulchral tobacco: ghosts, vandals?
Or maybe she guessed but maintained a tactful
silence. Full flavour blend, though, a mediocre
mixture, rather rough, Maryland: the red
working man's smoke, or so they say. Even the name
begets worn and wasted dreams: Parisienne,
girls cavorting on stage at the Moulin Rouge,
the lights of Pigalle, a century in mothballs, BB.
Or the looming, thoughtful face of
Jeanne Moreau: she would have liked
this tobacco. Today, though, five mallard
suddenly emerged from the bank
almost scaring me. Regally, they dropped into the water,
swimming against the feeble current, and for an instant
one of them turned.

BILANCIO DELLO SPERPERATORE

Tutte le mie ricchezze
le ho gettate al vento
in una sola notte
o forse due.

I talenti che avevo: sperperati.
Scomparse le onde del mio mare,
asciutti i fiumi. Le stelle
ho voluto spegnerle una dopo l'altra:
era un gioco. E ho regalato il buio
a un commerciante di luce.

Non ho tenuto fede
a nessuna promessa,
ho perso ogni cosa
con piena volontà.

A QUELLI CHE VERRANNO

Allora voi, che volgerete
lo sguardo verso di noi dalle vette
dei vostri tempi splendidi, come chi scruta una valle
che non ricorda neppure di avere percorsa:
non ci vedrete, dietro lo schermo di nebbie.
Ma eravamo qui, a custodire la voce.
Non ogni giorno e non in ogni ora
del giorno; qualche volta, soltanto,
quando sembrava possibile
raccogliere un po' di forza.
Ci chiudevamo la porta
dietro le spalle, abbandonando
le nostre case sontuose
e riprendevamo il cammino, senza meta.

THE SPENDTHRIFT TAKES STOCK

All my wealth
I have thrown to the wind
in a single night
or maybe two.

The talents that were mine: wasted.
The waves of my sea squandered,
the rivers dried up. The stars
I extinguished one after the other:
it was a game. And the darkness I gave
to a light salesman.

There is no promise
I have fulfilled.
I threw away everything
quite deliberately.

TO THOSE WHO COME AFTER

You, then, who will turn
your gaze on us from the summits
of your splendid times, like someone scanning a valley
he does not even remember passing through:
you will not see us, behind the screen of mist.
But we were here, custodians of the voice.
Not every day and not every hour
of the day; just sometimes,
when it seemed possible
to muster a little strength.
We closed the door
behind us, abandoning
our sumptuous houses
and resumed our way, directionless.

BOIS DE LA FOLIE

I

Ci sono i tronchi neri che salgono
con regolarità perfetta verso una volta cupa
e raggi gialli spiovono da intrichi
in larghe rose di luce;
al suolo, un misto
di foglie e legni marci. C'è il silenzio
delle castagne forate, dei ricci. Non si vedono
animali, uccelli. Non c'è niente di strano, o di inquietante.
Ma se uno gridasse,
dove andrebbe il suo urlo non si sa, forse sui rami
a penzolare giù come una sacca
oblunga, inconoscibile. Se il grido
non lo sente nessuno, cosa fa,
cosa diventa? Dove vanno
le grida inascoltate, che energia
sprigionano?

II

"Sono venuti due fiumi
uno a sinistra bianchissimo, vasto
fiume di luce bianca
e l'altro rapido
e magro,
uno era una donna vestita di chiaro
l'altro un'arma da taglio,
uno mi accarezzava i capelli
l'altro tagliava la gola,
uno cantava
l'altro aveva fame,
sono venuti due fiumi
io ero il mare
o l'abisso."

BOIS DE LA FOLIE

I

The black trunks ascend
in perfect order to a dark canopy
and yellow rays rain down though the tangle
in broad roses of light;
underfoot, a mixture
of leaves and rotten wood. The silence
of the worm-eaten chestnuts, the husks. No sign of
animals or birds. Nothing strange or disturbing.
But if someone were to cry out,
there is no knowing where his shout would go, maybe to hang down
from the branches like an oblong,
unrecognisable bag. If no one
hears the cry, what does it do,
what become? Where do unheard
cries go, what energy
do they unleash?

II

"There came two rivers
one on the left dazzling white, vast
river of white light
and the other quick
and thin,
one was a women brightly dressed
the other a bladed weapon,
one caressed my hair
the other cut my throat,
one sang
the other was famished,
there came two rivers
I was the sea
or the abyss."

III

"Abbiate cura degli argini,
se ancora lo potete. Custodite
i muri, i confini fragili.
Oltre è paura, e furia."

IV

"Non ho permesso a nessuno
di seguirmi fin qui.
Mai potrete sapere
che strada ho fatto o smarrito.
Musiche sorde
di trapano e scintille mi guidavano."

V

"Dopo la pianura, c'è soltanto pianura
e ancora pianura e pianura. Un grido
la percorre e si perde nel nulla."

VI

"La pallina metallica di un flipper
urta funghi e rimbalza via
verso altri funghi metallici,
altre luci cattive,
senza sapere che mano la spinge,
che volontà crudele,
che follia."

III

"Protect the dykes,
if you still can. Guard
the walls, the fragile borders.
Beyond is fear, and fury."

IV

"I have not let anyone
follow me this far.
You can never know
what road I have taken or lost.
The tuneless strains
of a drill and sparks were my guide."

V

"After the plain, there is nothing but plain,
plain and more plain. A cry
rings out and is lost in the emptiness."

VI

The metal sphere of a pinball machine
collides with mushrooms and rebounds
towards other metal mushrooms,
other menacing lights,
without knowing what hand drives it,
what cruel will,
what madness."

VII

"Guardateci e ammirate:
abbiamo piume azzurre velenose,
artigli e zanne lucenti, notti e notti
negli occhi e tra le mani
i sottili strumenti del piacere,
siamo i viandanti della pianura, i maleandanti,
inauditi premiamo ai confini,
disperati.

VIII

"Tutti i ponti sono stati distrutti
tutte le tigri sono state sguinzagliate."

IX

"Ferocia, sì. E le crepe
che spaccano il fango secco di questa pianura.
Via di qui, bastardi.
Via di qui."

MOVIMENTI ASCENSIONALI: LE SCALE DI ALBOGASIO

Case a strapiombo, asperità minori,
un figlio in testa; e, d'infilata, la breva
che prende il lago a sghimbescio, ingannatrice
si tuffa dalla Forca di San Martino,
costeggia rocce e strada e poi s'infuria
subito dopo Gandria, dove l'acqua s'allarga.

VII

"Observe us and admire:
we have poisonous pale-blue feathers,
gleaming claws and fangs, nights and nights
in our eyes, and in our hands
the sharp instruments of pleasure,
we are the wayfarers of the plain, the ill-farers,
appalling we press at the frontiers,
desperate."

VIII

"All the bridges are down
all the tigers have been unleashed."

IX

"Savagery, yes. And the cracks
that fissure the dry mud of this plain.
Get away, bastards.
Get away."

DESCENDING AND ASCENDING: THE STAIRWAYS OF ALBOGASIO

Houses overhanging, minor vexations,
a child in mind, across our beam the *breva* blowing,
taking the lake slantwise, treacherous,
swooping down from the Pass of San Martino,
skirting rock and roadway, then raging on
past Gandria, where the water widens.

È una sera di turbini, in cui scendo
come in un coro per le scale di un paese,
la mano alla barella, che altalena
e striscia lungo i muri, e ad ogni curva
stacca polvere bianca; ultima scorta
di calce per Erminia, la gentile
signora morta altrove, che ritorna
al suo balcone di minuscoli fiori.
Qui si passa nel buio: facendo presa
sullo scalino più basso con il piede,
per rampe verticali e stretti portici. Giù il lago
adesso non si vede, ma risuona
cupo dentro le darsene, e le barche
gemono nel loro cuore di legno e di catrame.
Qualche porta si schiude: chi s'affaccia
guarda in silenzio la nostra strana processione
che cala goffa agli inferi, alle nere
case del sonno. E tuttavia dal basso
sale qualcosa, un soffio umido e denso;
una mano d'aria o un gonfiore
s'insinua e chiede ascolto,
vita remota che risale dall'acqua, ancora informe
eppure già presente, già imperiosa
nel suo esistere scarno:
che incrocia noi in discesa e va più in alto,
come fumo sottile. Antiche scale
le scale d'Albogasio, su cui passano
ilari i vivi e i morti, salutandosi piano.

On this gusty evening, as if in a chorus,
I descend the village stairways,
bearing a stretcher, which sways
and scrapes along the walls, and at every turning
gouges out white powder; a last tribute
of lime for Erminia, the kind
lady who has died elsewhere and is now returning
to her balcony of tiny flowers.
Here we enter darkness: finding a footing
on the next step down as we negotiate
each steep flight and narrow portico. The lake below
is lost from view, but echoes
hollow in the boat-houses, and the boats
groan in their hearts of wood and pitch.
Doors half open and the occupants
silently observe our strange procession
as it makes its clumsy way to the netherworld,
to the black houses of sleep. And yet from below
something is rising, a dense wet breath;
a catspaw or swelling of the air
creeps up and demands a hearing,
distant life rising from the water, still shapeless
yet present, already imperious
in its bare existence:
it passes us coming down and continues upward,
like a wisp of smoke. Ancient stairways
the stairways of Albogasio, where dead and living
blithely rub shoulders, exchanging quiet greetings.

TREMOLÌO

I

In questa vasta desolazione di inverni

mentre la terra rannicchiata si torce
e qualcosa declina, che certi chiamano secolo
o con fierezza immotivata millennio,

e il signor Swatch propone un nuovo tempo
universale, rivoluzionario, che scandisca
il giorno in mille unità uguali per tutti,

e tutti finalmente saranno in orario
nelle rete, nel sacco, nel disastro
pilotato, felicemente privi di tempo o passato,

inutilmente tesi a un futuro virtuale
globale e inesistente, grazie al quale
la gleba del presente sarà lieve,

in questa vastissima desolazione di inverni,

mia nonna Idelma Formenti Bussolini
di anni novantanove, sorda quasi del tutto,
elusa la sorveglianza, è uscita sul balcone

e lì guarda e declama.

II

Davanti
trova quartieri su uno sfondo di nuvole,
finestre con donne affacciate di cui ignora

il nome, gli affanni, i piaceri; movimenti
incomprensibili di treni superveloci,
tessere magnetiche dello spessore di un'ostia,

TREMOR

I

In this vast desolation of winters,

while the crouched earth writhes
at the decline of what some call century
or with groundless pride millennium,

and Mr. Swatch proposes a revolutionary new
universal time that divides the day
into a thousand standard units,

and at last everyone will be on schedule
in the loop, in the bag, in the remote-controlled
disaster, blissfully deprived of time or past,

vainly awaiting a virtual, global
and non-existent future, thanks to which
the daily grind will be easy,

in this infinitely vast desolation of winters,

my grandmother Idelma Formenti Bussolini
aged ninety-nine, almost completely deaf,
having eluded her carers, comes out on the balcony,

looks and holds forth.

II

Before her
she finds apartment blocks against a background of clouds,
at windows women of whose names,

troubles and pleasures she knows nothing;
bewildering movements of high-speed trains,
magnetic cards thin as a communion wafer,

antenne paraboliche e intrecci di cavi; e là sopra,
sullo schermo dei cirri, fra tracce
di jumbolini e satelliti,

forse scorre in immagine un secolo suo,
in bianco e nero: carrette
di morti che passano lungo le vie di Lugano,

il padre che amava formaggio e buon vino,
l'avarizia dei ricchi, orologi
a molla montati e smontati, un odore di terra

e galline; Radamès, Rigoletto, le febbri
difteriche, il tifo, due guerre, zio Lampo,
Bergamo e i transatlantici, un'ernia,

il caffè della luna, frontiere, sfollati
e un corteggio di volti
ormai dimenticati e senza nome.

III

Si crede abbandonata sul balcone; se avesse letto
Ezra Pound penserebbe di essere Ezra Pound,
a strapiombo su Pisa,

ma è solo lei, la minuscola
scheggia, una lucertola
troppo vecchia per muoversi sul muro.

E dice cose insensate.
Allarma i vicini.
Grida al vento.

Sky TV aerials and skeins of cables; and up there,
on a screen of cirrus, amid the vapour trails
of executive jets and satellites,

maybe her century passes before her
in black and white: hearses
moving along the streets of Lugano,

her father who loved cheese and good wine,
the avarice of the rich, spring-driven
clocks assembled and dismantled, the smell of earth

and hens; Radamès, Rigoletto, diphtheria,
typhus, two wars, zio Lampo,
Bergamo and the transatlantic steamers, a hernia,

smuggled coffee, borders, evacuees
and a procession of faces
now forgotten and nameless.

III

She feels abandoned on the balcony. Had she read
Ezra Pound she might think she were Ezra Pound,
looking down on Pisa,

but it is only her, a tiny
splinter, a lizard
too old to run along the wall.

And she utters absurdities,
alarms the neighbours,
shouting in the wind's teeth.

IV

Si perde il suo delirio nella sera.
Le sue parole verranno raccontate a lungo
ridendo. Solo aria,

movimento dell'aria. Vano. Ma se un merlo
attardato, o il primo pipistrello del crepuscolo
le raccogliesse, quelle vibrazioni,

trasmettendole altrove, come un informe
ronzio; se quel ronzio, la pulsazione
debole del suo tempo provocasse

per vie traverse leggere alterazioni
elettromagnetiche, forse persino
un brevissimo sussulto di tensione,

se questo, che non si può escludere, avvenisse,
potremmo sperare che in un punto imprecisato
dello spazio, del nuovo spaziotempo, un terminale

anonimo, nel fondo di una stanza
o di un ufficio, visto o non visto, ronzante
in un bagliore azzurrino,

lampeggiasse per un attimo il suo estremo
ironico saluto: "e adesso, cari,
io vi lascio la mia buonanotte".

IV

Her ravings are lost in the evening.
They will laugh at her words long after.
Just air,

swirling air. Vanity. But if a belated
blackbird, or the first dusk-flying bat
were to pick up those vibrations,

transmit them elsewhere, like a formless
buzzing; if that buzzing, the weak pulsation
of her time, were in roundabout ways

to cause slight electro-magnetic
distortions, maybe even
a momentary surge in voltage,

were this to happen, and we cannot exclude it,
we could hope that at some indeterminate point
in space, the new space-time, an anonymous

terminal, at the back of a room
or office, visible or invisible, droning away
in a light-blue haze,

might for a moment flash up her final
ironic greeting: "and now, my dears,
I wish you goodnight".

from
FOLLA SOMMERSA
(2004)

SENZA TITOLO

Come le fragili piramidi di sasso
erette da qualcuno sulle montagne, dove i sentieri
sbucano finalmente a un pianoro,
a un passo, a una piccola cima. *A che scopo?*
Non chiederlo; sasso dopo sasso
costruisci anche tu quel che non serve
a nulla e a nessuno, ma è.
Forse verrà lo stambecco
ad annusare inquieto il tuo segnale;
sosterà per un attimo incerto
e poi salterà ancora fra le rocce
impraticabili, quasi verticali.
E lo potrò vedere, carezzare sul muso?
Verrà di notte o all'alba, e fuggirà. Ma sul terreno
lascerà un dono: minuscole palline
brune di sterco, e nell'aria un profumo selvaggio.

DUE AIRONI

I

Lago del Dosso, e nell'ambra dei prati
l'airone osserva immobile i canneti
e la nebbia, l'albergo in rovina,
l'erba folta, la stagione inoltrata e non mite,
le notizie non buone. Distante, cinereo,

from
**SUBMERGED MULTITUDE
(2004)**

UNTITLED

Like the fragile cairns of stones
built by someone in the mountains, where paths
lead finally to a plateau,
a pass or minor summit. *To what end?*
Do not ask; stone by stone
you too are building what profits
nothing and no one, but just is.
Maybe the wild goat will come
and warily sniff your signal;
he will stop for an instant uncertain
then continue his leaping on the impracticable,
almost vertical cliffs.
And shall I see him, rub his muzzle?
At night or dawn he will come, then flee. But on the ground
he will leave a gift: tiny brown
droppings, and on the air a scent of wilderness.

TWO HERONS

I

Lago del Dosso, and in the amber meadows
the motionless heron watches the reed beds
and the mist, the hotel in ruins,
the rank grass, the season late and inclement,
the news not good. Distant, ashen,

se ne va a larghi giri nel grigio, con ali
vaste che battono piano nell'aria,
senza emettere voce, pacifico, lugubre, inerme.
Più temibili voli s'avvitano
ai nostri cieli autunnali,
maschere e paradossi, altre macerie
e trappole di fuoco, petrolifere
giustizie micidiali.

II

Questo fila sull'acqua come freccia scura,
che sappia dove andare e perché:
l'airone grigio, cenere dell'alba, filamento
che viene sempre dalle brume più opache dell'ovest,
dalla notte, e vola dritto verso est, dove una luce
ancora vaga si dispone, e a sé lo attrae.
Più tardi arresta il volo in una valle nascosta,
e infine calmo ripiega le ali posando sul greto
di un torrentello che taglia i crinali con un tuffo
tra selve desuete e rocce vive, fili a sbalzo
cadenti, copertoni e fortunosi
argini o dighe: non vere cascate,
piccoli salti, al più, brevi riposi
d'acqua in pozzetti o conche fra le pietre o vasche
da canapa o da concia abbandonate, o sgrondi
utili forse un tempo, ora insensati, rozzi scivoli;
e qui, grigio nel grigio, scende a bere,
o a poca pesca, forse, timoroso
e attento, sempre vigile, prontissimo
a risalire rapido, silente,
il corpo e le zampe allungate, le ali svelte
a cogliere il vortice d'aria delle gole,
il soffio che lo conduce più all'interno di foreste,
nel cuore di mondi perduti,
verso un'acqua che scroscia dall'alto in minuscoli rivoli

it flies off in wide circles into the greyness,
vast wings slowly beating the air,
uttering no cry, pacific, mournful, meek.
More deadly flyers twist and turn
in our autumn skies,
masks and paradoxes, other wreckage
and fiery death-traps, murderous
acts of oil-fuelled justice.

II

This one glides over the water like a dark arrow,
which knows where to go and why:
the grey heron, ash of dawn, a thread
always issuing from the densest mists of the west,
out of the night, and flying due east, where a still faint light
spreads and draws it.
Later it halts its flight in a hidden valley
and calm at last folds its wings, landing on the gravel
of a torrent which crests ledges and dives down
through neglected woods and bare rocks,
decrepit cable-ways, old tyres and haphazard
banks or weirs: not real waterfalls,
short hops at most, brief resting places
of water in puddles or hollows between stones or basins
used for steeping hemp or tanning, or drains
maybe once useful, now crude pointless slipways;
and here, grey on grey, it stoops to drink,
or maybe fish a bit, cautious
and wary, always vigilant, ever ready
to take off again, rapid and silent,
body and legs drawn up in line, wings quick
to catch the updraught from gullies,
the breeze that takes it deeper into virgin forest,
to the heart of lost worlds,
to a stream that patters from above in tiny rivulets,

e sprofonda in terreni calcarei, marne bianche, e poi riemerge,
goccia nei prati, macchia o lieve alone
umido lungo il pallore di rocce friabili,
zampillo, occhio di lince.
E qui l'airone ti guida, qui ti lascia
stupito, a terra, e sale a picco oltre il suo zenith,
nel suo ignoto destino di bestia
timida, con le ali.

FOLLA SOMMERSA

> *La memoria non si oppone affatto all'oblio. I due termini che formano*
> *contrasto sono la cancellazione (l'oblio) e la conservazione ; la memoria*
> *è, sempre e necessariamente, un'interazione dei due.*
> Tzvetan Todorov, Memoria del male, tentazione del bene.
> Inchiesta su un secolo tragico.

Paul Hooghe, l'ultimo lanciere caduto su nessuna spiaggia, il superstite
delle trincee dimenticate e scomparse, su cui sorgono oggi
grandi complessi commerciali o lussuosi villaggi satellite
immersi nel verde di pitosfori, di platani le cui radici vagano
per antichi camminamenti sotterranei, il granatiere fantasma
ultracentenario spentosi a Bruxelles pochi mesi or sono,
come una piccola candela su cui passa il vento, che era stato
coscritto sedicenne di un secolo sedicenne (1916) eppure già
molto cattivo, molto crudele, ma si era ancora
al principio della sua storia,
alle vaghe promesse di stragi, alle belle bandiere: sapeva
di essere una curiosità, aspirava a un Guinness dei primati, a una targa?

E aveva memoria
lui, almeno lui, dei corpi nella notte e nel fango

is swallowed up by limestone or white marl, then re-emerges,
leeches into meadows, a stain or faint aura
of dampness against the pallor of crumbling rocks,
twinkling spring, eye of lynx.
Here the heron brings you, here leaves you
bewildered, earthbound, and rises steeply to its zenith,
obedient to its unknown destiny:
timorous beastie, but with wings.

SUBMERGED MULTITUDE

> *Remembering is not the opposite of forgetting. The two opposing terms are destruction and preservation (or "wiping" and "saving"): memory can only ever be the result of their interaction.*
> Tzvetan Todorov, *Hope and Memory.*
> *Reflections on the Twentieth Century.*

Paul Hooghe, last lancer not fallen on any beach, survivor
of the forgotten, long-gone trenches, on which now rise
great shopping malls or well-appointed satellite villages
immersed in the green of pittosporum and plane trees whose roots explore
old underground communication saps, the phantom
more-than-centenarian grenadier who passed away in Brussels
                                                a few months ago,
like a little candle snuffed out by the wind, sixteen-year-old
conscript of a sixteen-year-old century (1916) yet already
advanced in evil and cruelty, though this was just
the beginning of the story,
with its fine flags and vague promises of massacres : did he know
he was a curiosity, covet an entry in the Guinness Books of
                                                Records, a plaque?

And did he remember,
he at least, the torn, mutilated bodies in the night and mud,

straziati, mutilati, dei traccianti, sobbalzava, incompreso,
ripensando una mina saltare, una nube nervina ?
Quei morti gridavano ancora grazie a lui,
dalla Marna o sul Carso ?

O il nastro era già scorso, la pellicola
riavvolta e ormai illeggibile, tradotta
nel passato remoto dell'euro, o in un alzheimer? Ottant'anni,
secondo gli storici perdura la memoria
viva che il mondo ha di sé : poi è deportata
in un posto dove adesso c'è Paul Hooghe, coi suoi compagni,
i ricordi che forse aveva mio padre e quelli della sua età,
tra un po' ci sarà anche mio padre e tutti i suoi amici e nemici,
una grande folla sommersa che ci guarda in silenzio e ci attende.

LE PRIME FRAGOLE

Strisci nell'erba bianca di margherite.
Sei vestito di rosso, hai una cuffia rossa in testa,
e nella mano destra un pelacarote che infilzi
nel terreno ancora molle di marzo, sempre avanzando
lentamente nel folto del prato. Sdraiato
sull'erba, con le margherite negli occhi. Sto scalando
l'Everest, mi dici. E anche le guance sono rosse di gioia.

Strisciavi ieri nel tuo Everest di margherite
e io ti guardo oggi nel ricordo e intanto ascolto la radio
in attesa di notizie terribili, e tu continui a strisciare felice
e la radio dice della bambina schiacciata da un panzer a Gaza
tu prepari una pozione con piume d'uccello per imparare a volare
io ti preparo le prime fragole rosse dell'anno e mi chiedo se gli occhi
dell'uomo che guidava il panzer avranno capito.

the tracer shells; did he start up, misunderstood,
recalling the explosion of a mine, a cloud of nerve gas?
Did those dead men still cry out, thanks to him,
from the Marne or on the Carso?

Or was the tape already played, the film
rewound and now illegible, translated
into the past historic of the euro, or Alzheimer's? Eighty years,
according to historians, is the duration of society's
living memory: then it is deported
to the place where Paul Hooghe is now, with his companions,
the memories maybe retained by my father and those of his age,
soon my father, too, and all his friends and enemies will be there,
a submerged multitude silently watching and waiting for us.

FIRST STRAWBERRIES

You crawl in grass white with daisies,
dressed in red and wearing a red bobble-hat,
with a potato peeler in your right hand
to stick in the still soft March earth, slowly advancing
in the thick of the meadow. Face down
in the grass, with daisies in your eyes. I'm climbing
Everest, you tell me, even your cheeks red with joy.

Yesterday you were crawling in your Everest of daisies
and today I see you in memory while listening to the radio
expecting dreadful news, and you crawl on happily
and the radio reports on a little girl crushed by a tank in Gaza
you prepare a potion with feathers to make you fly
I prepare the year's first red strawberries and wonder if the eyes
of the man driving the tank took it in.

SENZA IMMAGINI

Avendo da anni deciso felicemente
di rinunciare alla televisione non vedremo
la danza delle bombe su Bagdad su Bassora sui resti
di quello che un tempo fu il centro del mondo.
Non vedremo le facce gravi dei potenti
le smorfie eroiche degli inviati speciali
le scene raccapriccianti di macelli e di fuoco. No, grazie,
rinunceremo allo spettacolo. Alla festa.
Davanti alla radio, in silenzio,
potremo guardare nel vuoto, immaginare
quel che si può immaginare, troppo poco.

Senza immagini
tutto sarà più chiaro, più tremendo.

LETTERA DA NIKOLAJEVKA

Sento urlare in tutti i dialetti, è un urlo solo.
                                                    Nuto Revelli

Se c'è stata una colpa, credo,
dico di noi fuscelli,
è stata l'ignoranza. Il non potere,
il non volere capire. Trascinati
da un vento troppo forte, e ogni domanda
era domanda d'ansia : ci bastava
un urlo di risposta, un po' di caldo.
Non solo allora, sempre, chi ne è uscito:
l'abitudine
a chinare la testa, o a rialzarla
solo in un moto d'ira rovinoso. Ma voi, adesso,
siete molto diversi? Te lo chiedo
davvero, te lo chiedo

WITHOUT IMAGES

Having years ago happily decided
to give up television we shall not see
the dance of bombs on Baghdad on Basra on the remains
of what was once the centre of the world.
We shall not see the grave features of the powerful
the heroic grimaces of the special correspondents
the horrific scenes of fire and slaughter. No, thank you,
we shall do without the spectacle. The party.
Sitting by the radio, in silence,
we can stare into space, imagine
what can be imagined, all too little.

Without images,
all will be clearer, more dreadful.

LETTER FROM NIKOLAJEVKA

> *I hear screaming in all dialects, a single scream.*
> Nuto Revelli

If we dry husks
were guilty of anything,
it was, I think, ignorance. Not being able
or willing to understand. Driven
by a wind too strong, and every question
was born of anxiety: enough for us
an answering shout, a bit of warmth.
Not only then, but always, for those who came through it:
the habit
of bowing the head, or raising it
only in a flash of violent anger. But you, now,
are you any different? I ask you this
seriously, I ask

sapendo già che non potrai rispondere,
che non vorrai rispondere temendo
di sbagliare, o di ferirmi
ancora. Ma è questa
l'unica nostra speranza, brucia e insiste
qui, sotto neve e fango, sola brace.
Altri capirono, forse, non noi: colpa e condanna,
ecco l'eredità. Questa manciata
di terra magra e povera, un passato
di fumo. Raccoglietelo nel palmo di una mano,
fate fiorire qualcosa di non guasto,
se può crescere ancora. Diffidate
d'ogni risposta. Con fiducia e sospetto
riscattateci. Capite anche per noi, se lo potete.

DEPOSIZIONE

Rosso su azzurro e tratti bruni e il bianco,
tutti colori metallici. Il giorno
si apre così, sopra una costa
desolata di merci e portuali, ed è una danza
di morte ad Algesiras.
No che non è il Pontormo : il furgoncino
si spalanca, offre il suo carico di casse (Primeurs),
tangerine e cadaveri. Fissa nel gesto, l'ultimo, una mano
magrebina, e poi il candore,
la smorfia d'asfissia.
Dietro, altri quattro, attorcigliati. Impianto
difettoso, fuga di gas, clandestini.
Forze di polizia.

already knowing you cannot answer, fearing
lest you get it wrong, or wound me
again. But this
is our only hope, burning and persisting
here, under snow and mud, a mere ember.
Others understood maybe, not us: guilt and condemnation
are our legacy. This handful
of thin, poor soil, a past
gone up in smoke. Gather it in the palm of your hand,
cultivate something unspoiled,
if it still can grow. Distrust
every answer. With trust and suspicion
redeem us. Understand for us, too, if you can.

DEPOSITION

Red on blue and streaks of brown, and white,
all metallic colours. So dawns
the day over a desolate quayside
of goods in transit and dock workers, and a dance
of death at Algesiras.
No, this is no Pontormo: the truck doors
yawn open, revealing a load of boxes (*Primeurs*),
tangerines and corpses. Frozen in gesture, the last of them,
a Moroccan hand, then the whiteness,
the grimace of asphyxiation.
Behind him, another four, twisted together. Faulty
generator, leak of gas, illegal immigrants.
Squads of police.

GIUDIZIO UNIVERSALE

Ah, non si fanno certo più illusioni
gli stornelli di Berna, che riparano per freddo
tempo nel timpano fra le gambe dei dannati e dei santi,
tra papi d'oro e imperatori rimasti di stucco,
e una schiera di più anonimi pedoni, sotto code
di rosso drago o lustri ottoni celesti, indifferenti
tanto alle fiamme che ai solluccheri dell'eden: caldo è caldo,
diranno, e non dipende, perdio, dal paradiso
o dall'inferno; ne sanno qualcosa colombi e piccioni
troppo paffuti e tondi per ascendere
a così comodo nido, circonfuso
di reti quasi invisibili, ma non prive di buchi.

SCIAME IN FUGA

Sciamavano le vespe – mietitrebbia
sconvolgevano i campi, nidi a pezzi –
in furioso ronzio.
Per giorni, sin dall'alba le sentivi
dietro le zanzariere del casale
sui colli, a Mazzangrugno. Un'ombra al vetro,
un sommesso raspare, e quel brusio
migrante, minaccioso e forse solo
lamento : nelle celle, fra i cardi,
quali pupe, o ricordi, e che speranze
d'amore e sonno dolce
custodivano invano ? Cingoli e ferro,
l'attimo che disintegra, e lo sciame
si disperde nel vento, in mezzo a nuvole
di polvere rossastra
e poi va via : verso altri campi, o boschi, verso mari
mai visti, dentro una storia altrui
che stringe e sforza

LAST JUDGEMENT

Ah yes, they cherish no illusions
the starlings of Berne, sheltering from the cold
in the tympanum 'twixt legs of saints and sinners,
gilded popes and dumbstruck emperors,
and a shower of more anonymous buggers, 'neath tails
of red dragon or bright celestial brasses, indifferent
equally to flames of hell and joys of eden: snug is snug,
they would say, and does not depend, for goodness' sake, on paradise
or inferno; go and ask the doves and pigeons
too plump and portly to accede
to so comfortable a roost, protected
by netting almost invisible but not devoid of holes.

DISPLACED SWARM

The wasps were swarming – combines
devastating the fields, nests in pieces –
in a buzzing fury.
For days, from first light, you could hear them
at the mesh screens of the farmhouse
in the hills, at Mazzangrugno. A shadow on the glass,
subdued scratching, and that hum,
migrant, menacing and maybe only
a lament: in their cells, among the thistles,
like pupae, or memories, and what hopes
of love and sweet sleep
did they nourish in vain? Flailing metal,
the moment of disintegration, and the swarm
disperses on the wind, in clouds
of reddish dust
and off it goes: to other fields, or woods, or unknown
seas, become part of someone else's story
which constrains and forces,

e sembra persa e cattiva.
Api nemiche o fiaccole di pece,
una memoria irta di veleno
o la smemoria torbida del vino
sotto un bicchiere arrovesciato e il fumo
che sale adagio e paralizza e uccide.

Tre giorni rimasero sui vetri. Poi, d'improvviso,
un mattino scomparvero.

CONCOMITANZE

Rieccola. Ha socchiuso
i vetri del balcone, e sta fumando. Si distingue
appena il fumo azzurro che risale
nell'aria, verso i tetti e le case più alte. Di lei
non so nulla: appare
nella penombra di una tenda, e fuma.

Forse interrompe qualcosa,
o la disturba l'odore. O ha dei figli, un marito
che vieta. Fuma e guarda, penso,
perdutamente: un camion che posteggia,
le ambulanze, l'ingiallita
sorte di un tiglio cittadino. La ritrovo
laggiù ad ogni pausa che concedo
a me, se studio o leggo. E a volte credo
che anche lei abbia notato
le nostre concomitanze. Che si chieda
chi è quel tizio che ogni tanto si affaccia
e sta lì a rimirare i palazzi. Magari
potremmo un giorno salutarci con la mano,
come dal ponte di due navi che si incrociano
in mezzo al vasto mare. Ciao, ciao,

anticipating loss and suffering.
Hostile bees or smouldering torches,
memory shot through with venom
or the turbid forgetfulness of wine
under an upturned glass and the smoke
that rises slowly to paralyse and kill.

Three days they remained on the panes. Then, suddenly,
one morning they were gone.

CONCOMITANCES

There she is again. She has half closed
the balcony doors, and is smoking. You can just make out
the pale blue smoke rising
into the air, towards the roofs and the houses higher up. I know
nothing about her: she appears
in the shadow of a curtain, and smokes.

Maybe she is taking a break from something,
or doesn't like the smell. Or she has children, an anti-smoking
husband. She smokes and watches, I think,
absent-minded: a lorry parking,
ambulances, the yellowed
fate of an urban lime-tree. I find her
there every time I allow myself a break,
whether studying or reading. And sometime I believe
that she too has noticed
our concomitances. That she wonders
who that chap is who now and again appears
and stands there surveying the apartment buildings. One day
we might even wave to each other,
as if from the decks of two ships passing
in the middle of the vast ocean. Hello, hello,

vorrebbe dire il gesto, ciao, buona fortuna,
chiunque tu sia, dovunque tu vada.
E buon coraggio, anche, sulle strade
che ti portano. Davvero,
sarebbe bello salutarsi così. Darebbe forza.

I GIORNI SONO PIENI DI CAVERNE E DI TIGRI

Se il ramo incagliato tra i sassi è giunto a valle
dopo un aspro tragitto,
e lo sollevi tu
come un trofeo di caccia, da dipingere
di rosso e giallo,
i colori della tigre e del drago;
se il piatto della pietra
ti narra la sua storia di pelliccia
di lupo grigio
o di naufragio sulle coste
del mare di Lugano che sarebbe
poi lago ma non è;
se in verità volevo scrivere di te
un'altra cosa che sembrava così chiara, cristallina,
e invece anche in pensiero
riesci a far confusione, e non stai mai
giudizioso e tranquillo; vorrà dire
che il mondo è più squillante e avventuroso,
le notti lunghe di grida
e i giorni pieni di caverne e di tigri,
dove molto coraggio ci vuole per entrare
in cerca di un ramo d'oro o di una pietra
luminosa, ametista o tormalina.

the gesture would mean, hello, good luck,
whoever you are, wherever you are going.
And be of good courage, too, on the roads
you must follow. Really
it would be nice to exchange such greetings. Strengthening.

DAYS FULL OF CAVES AND TIGERS

If the branch caught among the boulders has reached us
after a rough and stormy passage,
and you retrieve it
like a hunting trophy, to paint
in red and yellow,
colours of the tiger and the dragon;
if the stone's flat surface
tells a story of grey
wolf skin
or of shipwreck on the shores
of the Lugano Sea, which they wrongly claim
to be a lake;
if really my intention was to write something else
about you that seemed so crystal clear,
but even in my mind
you manage to confuse it, and you are never
sensible and good as gold; it must mean
the world is more jazzy and exciting,
the nights long with shouting
and the days full of caves and tigers,
where great courage is needed to enter
in quest of golden bough or sparkling
gemstone, amethyst or tourmaline.

DOPO TRENT'ANNI

Ti seguo da trent'anni mentre vaghi cercando
non sai nemmeno cosa. Sono la luce
di un'esplosione lontana, il tuo sole di ghiaccio,
due occhi spalancati sulla magrezza di un male
che apriva certe porte, o prospettive di fuga.
Diversamente: era questo l'indizio,
la rifrazione del mio raggio sulla superficie del mondo.
Voleva dire distruggere
frugare fra gli scarti. Spossessarsi.
Voleva dire camminare con gli occhi bendati.

Ti seguo da trent'anni alta come un rapace
con il mio becco duro di nibbio, la mia vista
che sa distinguere un topolino fra le rocce
o la tua traccia barcollante sui sentieri.
Ero nei sogni che non potevi ricordare.
Ero un grido prima dell'alba, una porta chiusa,
uno zigomo che affiora sulla pelle. Il volto folle di un uomo
impiastricciato di sugo, pulsante. Ero il bagliore
di una vallata percorsa da un fiume, luccicante di fuochi.
Ero un tumore e una stella.

E non potevi guardarmi: accecavo.
Adesso, guarda. Guarda il tronco
contorto di questi ulivi che si annodano
al terreno sassoso. Guarda il mare e la costa
incisa, e il vento scuotere
ogni ramo. È la mia ala,
non medica, ti porta, ti sostiene.
Fa quasi giorno, e un'ombra, la tua ombra
striscia tra i rampicanti e le prime formiche. Solo un'ombra,
il poco che ti resta. La tua luce a rovescio.

Sono qui, per un istante posata : a rincuorarti
e a toglierti ogni speranza. Non c'è pace
nel corso delle cose e dei corpi, ma una pace
diversa brilla ovunque e ci chiama. Se vibra

THIRTY YEARS ON

Thirty years I have followed as you wander seeking
you know not what. I am the light
of a distant explosion, your ice sun,
two eyes wide open to the emaciation of a sickness
that opened certain doors, or prospects of escape.
Differently: this was the pointer,
the refraction of my ray on the surface of the earth.
It meant destroying,
digging among the rubbish. Forsaking possessions.
It meant walking blindfold.

Thirty years I have followed you high as a raptor
with my hard kite's beak and eye
that can make out a mouse among the rocks
or your unsteady track along the pathway.
I was in the dreams you could not recall.
I was a cry before dawn, a locked door,
a cheek bone breaking the skin. The insane face of a man
plastered with tomato sauce, pulsating. I was the gleam
of a river in a valley, twinkling with lights.
I was a tumour and a star.

And you could not look at me: so blinding was I.
Look now. Look at the contorted
trunk of these olive trees that knit
to the stony ground. Look at the sea and the jagged
coastline, and the wind shaking
every branch. It is my wing,
not healing, but bearing and sustaining you.
It is almost day, and a shadow, your shadow
glides among the climbers and the first ants. Just a shadow,
the little left to you. Your light in reverse.

I am here, perched for an instant: to hearten you
and take away all hope. There is no peace
in the course of things and bodies, but a different peace
shines everywhere and calls us. If the soft breath of time

sopra l'acqua o sull'erba il soffio lieve
del tempo: ecco steli dispersi, sradicati, ed ecco il turbine
leggero delle foglie che s'infiammano
e svaniscono. Guardami pure, adesso, non abbaglio.
Abbandonarsi e resistere, due fasi
identiche del sangue e del respiro, dell'inchiostro
e del foglio, come sai. Cammina, scrivi.

IN CAMMINO

I

Era un pensiero, un amico? Era un'ombra
a tenerci per mano, a condurre. Con tenacia
toglieva una pietra, indicava il sentiero. Una piccola luce,
uno zufolo, non una tromba
d'oro.

Scomparsa, poi. D'improvviso: un affondo
di pesce svanito nel nulla, o fiocinato. Sull'acqua una striscia
più scura, qualcosa che impallidisce. Il viaggio
continua, irragionevole. Lambisce l'acqua, l'ombra,
sale ancora.

II

Quello che torna è il vuoto, come sai. Le cose zitte
blindate in un silenzio quasi ostile, e l'occhio inerte
che non sa più guardare. Un deserto
popoloso, un rumore. Dentro le mani cosa stringi?
I solchi incavati del palmo, un destino ridicolo.
Una volta si correva a perdifiato, ore di corsa,

vibrates over the water or over the grass:
here are scattered, uprooted stalks, and here the faint
whirlwind of leaves that flare up
and vanish. So look at me now, I no longer dazzle.
Surrender and resistance, two identical
phases of blood and breathing, of ink
and paper, as you well know. Walk on, and write.

MOVING ON

I

Was it a thought, a friend? It was a shade
that held our hand, led us. With firmness
it removed a stone, pointed the pathway. A tiny light,
a penny whistle, not a golden
trumpet.

Then disappeared. Suddenly: like a fish
vanished into the depths, or harpooned. On the water a darker
trace, something melting away. The journey
continues, senseless. Touches the water, the shadow,
rises again.

II

What returns is emptiness, as you know. The voiceless things
armoured in an almost hostile silence, and the inert eye
no longer able to see. A crowded
desert, a noise. What are you clasping in your hand?
The sunken furrows of the palm, a ridiculous destiny.
Once we ran at breakneck speed, ran for hours,

e quando uno cedeva gli altri intorno
correvano per lui, ridando lena. La meta
era lì, correre insieme, non altro.
Correre insieme. Forse
anche adesso, solitari, siamo
insieme ad altri lontani che corrono
testardi. Passano concentrati
lungo le strade e le generazioni,
e vanno. E intanto ascoltano
il ritmo, e se mai un'eco
d'altri venisse a loro, come un vento leggero,
un richiamo. Messageri
anonimi, dispersi, di poche parole.
Li riconoscono i bambini,
e anche certi animali che li seguono
per un tratto, gioiosi.
Criniere d'aria, fiato. Dunque vai
con loro, che non sempre puoi vedere,
al tuo più lento passo,
uno fra i tanti.

and when one tired the others around
ran for them, taking the strain. That was the point,
to run together, nothing else.
To run together. Maybe
even now, on our own, we are
together with others far away who run
obstinately. Absorbed, they pass
along the roads and generations,
and move on. And meanwhile they listen for
the rhythm, and whether perchance some echo
of others might reach them, like a light breeze,
a reminder. Anonymous
messengers, scattered, of few words.
Children recognise them,
and some animals which follow them
for a stretch, joyful.
Ripples of wind, breath. Go with them,
then, whom you cannot always see,
at your slower pace,
one among so many.

from
CORPO STELLARE
(2011)

CON PICCOLE ALI

Sul Po, sotto Superga,
tutto pareva notte, il fiume e il tempo
scivolavano muti. Per viali
di traffico e stanchezze
si risaliva il buio, controcorrente
senza particolari prospettive.
Ma breve un segno sull'acqua
significava sorpresa, bianca scia.
Canoe, due scafi lesti, l'allegria
gorgheggia, ti sfiora per caso
e va, nelle sere più cupe,
con piccole piccole ali.

APRILE 2006. CARTOLINE D'ITALIA

1

Sperando in una luce lontana guardavano i figli
e i figli dei figli perduti di lingua e costume
sbucciavano povere arance, raccoglievano
cauti le poche briciole dal tavolo
vuotavano sempre il bicchiere fino all'ultima
goccia di sangue nero.

In ginocchio dentro cunicoli di molti padroni,
su strade assolate di porfido e asfalto, praterie

from
**HEAVENLY BODY
(2011)**

ON TINY WINGS

Along the Po, below Superga,
all seemed like night, the river and time
gliding silent. Through congested
streets with weary tread
breasting the current of darkness
with no special prospects.
But a sudden sign on the water
signalled surprise, a white wake.
Canoes, two quicksilver hulls, mirth
bubbles up, touches you by chance
and flies, even on the darkest evenings,
on tiny, tiny wings.

APRIL 2006. POSTCARDS OF ITALY

1

Hoping in a distant light they looked to their children
and children's children lost to language and custom
they peeled poor oranges, warily
collected the few crumbs from the table
always emptied the glass to the last drop
of black blood.

On their knees in the pit-shafts of many masters,
on sun-baked roads of clinker and asphalt, prairies

da imbrigliare, concimi, dritti fino al silicio
del bronco, all'artrosi, alla falce.
Dimenticateci, dicevano,
lasciateci andare per sempre
nel solco del nostro silenzio rassegnato.
Siamo enfisemi, escrescenze del tempo.
Veniamo da boschi che non esistono più, da antiche case
di fumo che diventano posteggi, supermarket
in cui ci smarriremmo,
vagando giorni e giorni tra le merci. Lascateci andare.
Furono dighe, trafori, mine, vie ferrate,
più tardi autostrade, fabbriche,
ma ancora uno stesso abbandono, un'identica forza
di spalle e teste basse, uffici consolari,
dialetti alle caviglie
come piombi. Le mani talvolta stringevano
manciate di terra, annusando
un odore d'infanzia, cipolle
smarrite nei secoli, animali già morti
prima ancora di nascere.

Terra nera del Belgio o d'oltremare,
terra grassa d'Argovia o di Germania,
zolle argentine, torbe : ma un odore
riportava ogni volta a quel paese
di cui si era imparato a fare senza,
limone sfiorito, spento
limone rubato.

Furono dimenticati, proprio come volevano. Poi i figli
generarono figli, i nipoti pronipoti, pizzerie, piccole imprese,
lauree, discendenze. Imparando a dire no in lingue diverse,
e a dire grazie, mi scusi, ho fame, esisto anch'io.
Potendo scegliere
alcuni scelsero, infine. Oggi rimandano
al paese lontano immemore, come un grano portato dal vento,
la cosa di cui il paese non aveva più quasi coscienza :

to be tamed, fertilisers, leading straight to
silicosis, arthritis, the reaper's sickle.
Forget us, they said
let us go forever
in the furrow of our resigned silence.
We are emphysemas, excrescences of time.
We come from woods that are no more, smoky
old houses become car parks, supermarkets
in which we would get lost,
wandering for days among the shelves. Let us go.
Their destiny was dams, tunnels, mines, railroads,
later motorways, factories,
but still the same surrender, the same effort
of shoulders and bowed heads, consulates,
dialects dogging their heels
like ball-and-chain. Their hands sometimes grasped
handfuls of earth, sniffing
a scent of childhood, onions
lost in the centuries, animals dead
even before birth.

Black soil of Belgium or lands overseas,
rich soil of Aargau or Germany,
Argentinian sod, peat: but some smell
harked back each time to that country
they had learned to do without,
lemon tree faded, withered,
lemon stolen.

They were forgotten, just as they willed. Then their children
bore children, their grandchildren great-grandchildren, pizzerias,
                                                  small businesses,
degrees, descendants. Learning to say no in different languages,
to say thank you, excuse me, I'm hungry, I too have my place.
Allowed to choose
some chose, at last. Today they remit
to the distant unmindful country, like a seed on the wind,
the thing that country had almost consigned to oblivion:

che sorpresa ! arriva dall'estero, sui giorni italiani umiliati,
un po' di civile decenza, la nemesi degli emigrati.

2

Dopo Marzabotto, quando la strada si inerpica
verso il bastione d'Appennino, lungo il Setta, un solitario
uccello di larghe ali volteggiava
sopra l'ingorgo, lento.
Irraggiungibile, per ore, Pian del Voglio:
autotreno di sbieco ostruiva, forse morti.
Così spiegava almeno da un furgone
un uomo mite, e poi cercava di calmare
dolcissimo un ragazzo tetraplegico
ancorato al sedile, che gridava.

Improvvisata piazza, l'autostrada
si affolla, astiosa: chi telefona o fuma,
qualcuno che fotografa un paesaggio
inconsueto, un altro resta
in auto mentre intinge dei biscotti
in una crema scura, ascolta techno
e il rombo di un motore incattivito.
Eccoci qua, prigione di noi stessi,
privi di scelta, stretti fra attesa e sospetto,
chiusi al viaggio e sordi alla vergogna.

Alto sui muraglioni
correva un pendolino per Bologna.

3

Basta un raggio di sole per accendere
i pesci e gli animali sulle rive: e come splendono
le foglioline più chiare, e quelle pieghe

Surprise, surprise! from abroad, in the day of Italy's humiliation, returns
a hint of civic decency, the emigrants' revenge.

2

After Marzabotto, when the road climbs towards
the bastion of the Appennines, along the Setta, a solitary
raptor circled on broad wings
above the snarl-up, slowly.
Unreachable, for hours, Pian del Voglio:
blocked by skewed artic, maybe victims.
This at least the explanation of a mild chap
in a van, who tried ever so gently
to calm a tetraplegic boy
strapped into a seat, shouting.

Improvised city square, the motorway
seethes with irritation: people phoning or smoking,
taking pictures of an unfamiliar
landscape, one individual stays
in his car dunking biscuits
in a dark creamy liquid, listening to techno
and the roar of an engine in need of tuning.
Here we are, then, prison of ourselves,
stripped of choice, caught between waiting and suspicion,
dead to travel, deaf to shame.

High up on its embankment
sped a bullet train to Bologna.

3

It takes only a sunray to light up
the fish and the animals on the banks: how they shine
the lighter bits of foliage, and those folds

di marmo sulla smorfia dei dannati,
il bianco e le creature
d'Orvieto. Ma nel bar
proni sopra i pulsanti, ragazzini
muovono calciatori virtuali, e ad ogni azione
s'illumina lo schermo d'un boato dagli spalti.
Anche mio figlio
è con loro stavolta; ma non sa
a cosa corrisponde il tasto verde, o quello blu,
e lo chiede lieto
ai suoi nuovi compagni. Che lo guardano
attoniti, di colpo senza voce.
Ma sei straniero, dicono, *non sai
neanche come si gioca?* E il loro dubbio
tecnico, non linguistico
pare a me atroce

4

Nella via Deliziosa
si ritiene abbia vissuto il Perugino,
proprio quando cercava gli accenti
nuovi del verde e segni
di speranza. Una bottega
artigiana adesso disperata espone meste
scritte e disegni: *sono ladri, bugiardi, e se ne vantano.*
Questo bisogna dire: sono ladri,
ministri e presidente.
E nessuno lo dice, se ne fregano
di tutto, tutti al soldo del padrone.
Ma io sono un coglione,
e di questo mi vanto.

of marble on the grimacing faces of the damned,
the whiteness and the creatures
of Orvieto. But in the bar
hunched over the controls, boys
manœuvre virtual soccer players, and at each move
the screen lights up with a roar from the terraces.
On this occasion my son
has joined them; but does not know
what the green button is for, or the blue one,
and blithely asks
his new companions. They look at him
amazed, suddenly speechless.
What! Are you a foreigner, they say, *you can't even
play the game?* And their doubt
– technical not linguistic –
seems to me atrocious.

4

Perugino, they say, lived here
in the Via Deliziosa,
when he was searching for new
shades of green and shoots
of hope. Desperate
a craft boutique now displays pathetic
inscriptions and drawings: *they are thieves, liars, and proud of it.*
This needs to be said: president
and ministers are thieves.
And no one says so, they don't give a damn
about anything, all with their snouts in the trough.
But I'm a pillock,
and proud of it.

5

Chi è questo che fuma accanto a me
il suo mezzo toscano tra mezze parole
di convenienza, e sorride
nell'aria tremolante del mattino, dà uno sguardo
ai tetti, alle donne che passano, alle nuvole,
ripiega il suo giornale di rapina, alza la testa
e si avvia con la moglie col fare di chi
ha vinto ancora, come sempre sa
di avere vinto: e vinto cosa poi?

Lui è lui, io forse io, nessuno è noi.

LETTERE DA BABEL

I

Dici di avere sognato un sogno orribile. In TV
ci vedevi morire sepolti fra macerie, ed era lunga la scena, interminabile,
ripetuta più volte: il grande crollo della torre di Babele,
e noi là sotto, bianca polvere mediatica. Tu
venivi poi affidato a governanti severissime,
teutoniche o anglosassoni, cattive. Noi dispersi.
Aggiungi, ma non c'entra, che vorresti
forse impegnare i tuoi risparmi per un nuovo videogioco
che ha un nome sorprendente: PANDORA TOMORROW. E siccome
non sai nulla o quasi nulla di Pandora ti racconto
l'invidia degli dei per noi imperfetti
testardi esseri umani,
mangiatori di pane, sensibili alla bellezza. E ancora giorni
si susseguono, viaggi, e sempre quel tuo sogno mi accompagna,
in segreto, e non capisco perché; finché guidando

5

Who is this man here beside me smoking
his small Tuscan cheroot and making
small talk? He smiles
in the shimmering morning air, glances
at the rooftops, the passing women, the clouds,
folds his commandeered newspaper, lifts his head
and strolls off with his wife with the air of
a winner, who knows he is always a winner:
but what in fact has he won?

He is what he is, I maybe me, no one is us.

LETTERS FROM BABEL

I

You say you dreamed a horrible dream. On TV
you saw us die, buried in rubble, and the scene went on endlessly,
repeated over and over: the great collapse of the Tower of Babel,
and us beneath the media dust cloud. Then
you were put in the care of tyrannical guardians,
Teutonic or Anglo-Saxon, nasty. Parents missing.
You add, though it's not relevant, that you might like
to spend the money you have saved on a new video-game
with a surprising name: PANDORA TOMORROW. And since
you know next to nothing about Pandora I tell you about
the gods' envy of us imperfect
stubborn human beings,
bread-eaters, sensitive to beauty. And so the days
go by and, on my travels, still that dream of yours stays with me
hidden away, and I don't know why; until driving

nel traffico tra Modena e Bologna, mentre uno sciame
di passeri sale su da dietro un muro come un vento di mare,
anche le immagini cominciano a volare in una sola direzione,
come i passeri, confuse eppure unite, non senza un po' di grazia
e di paura. C'è qualcosa
di vero nel tuo sogno, una visione
nitida che ci sfugge. E per questo ti scrivo. Perché so,
adesso so, che siamo qui davvero, io e tua madre,
e ci teniamo per mano in mezzo a tutte queste macerie
di una cosa che non è crollata ancora, ma vacilla
e forse un giorno crollerà. Chiamala Europa, o mondo,
o solo un altro sogno; e forse è l'ombra di un secolo e di un vuoto
che abbiamo visto e sperato di cancellare con la gioia.
Un pezzetto di gioia per ciascuno: era questo il disegno,
niente di complicato. Un poco a tutti. Da qui ti scriviamo,
e siamo in molti, segnati da riso e mestizia. Altri parlavano
delle grandi vittorie, di rinascite. Noi sappiamo da tempo : la sconfitta,
questo era il vero punto di partenza. Dovere di memoria e speranza,
diritto alla felicità sempre negata, sempre da costruire. E la vergogna,
anche, da non dimenticare: tutto ciò che era stato, e non doveva
essere mai, mai più. Ieri la voce
più alta di Sarajevo diceva, la mano sul cuore: sono stato
parte di una speranza collettiva, era un progetto
da oceano a steppa, vasto come il vento, ed è crollato. Posso solo
alzare la mano sinistra, nera di tristezza,
la destra non si apre più, chiusa in un grido
che salda le unghie alla carne, la Bosnia all'Europa che cade.

II

Qui ci sono terrazze, balaustre a cui appoggiarsi, carissimo figlio,
sporte sulla pianura ; guardiamo le strade uguali, monocordi,
il flusso ordinato del traffico e dei giorni, il tuo futuro,
e non siamo sicuri di niente. Ma speriamo.
Assurdamente, speriamo. Il fuoco è acceso.

in traffic between Modena and Bologna, as a flock
of sparrows takes to the air from behind a wall like wind off the sea,
the images, too, begin to fly in a single direction,
like the sparrows, confused but united, not without a touch of grace
and fear. There's something
true in your dream, a clear vision
that escapes us. And that's why I'm writing. Because I know,
I know now, that we are really here, your mother and I,
holding hands amid all this wreckage
of a thing that has not yet collapsed, but is tottering
and may one day fall. Call it Europe, or the world,
or just another dream; and maybe it's the shadow of a century and an
                                                                                                 emptiness
that we saw and hoped to fill with joy.
A little bit of joy for each person: this was the plan,
nothing complicated. Something for everyone. From here we write to you,
and there are many of us, marked by sadness and laughter. Others spoke
of great victories, renaissances. We have known for years: defeat,
this was the real starting point. The duty to remember and to hope,
the right to happiness always denied, always to be constructed. And
                                                                                                 the shame,
too, not to be forgotten: everything that had been, and must not
happen ever, ever again. Yesterday the highest voice
of Sarajevo said, hand on heart: I was
part of a collective hope, a project
from ocean to steppe, vast as the wind, and it has crumbled. I can only
raise my left hand, black with sadness,
my right will no longer open, clenched in a cry
that welds the nails to the flesh, Bosnia to falling Europe.

II

Here there are terraces, balustrades to lean on, dearest son,
overlooking the plain; we survey the uniform, monochord roads,
the ordered flow of traffic and the days, your future,
and we are not sure of anything. But we hope.
Absurdly, we hope. The fire is lit.

Dita come farfalle
corrono sopra le corde di molte chitarre, strane lingue
s'incrociano, bisticciano e si sfiorano, canzoni
passano lente o veloci attraverso i cieli, il vino è buono.
Adesso siamo seduti su un ponte fra rive invisibili,
sopra un fiume che luccica e canta, e si sorride.

Domani, poco prima dell'alba, quando affiorano i pesci
e guizzano sull'acqua luminosi, con un battito d'ali Pandora
scivolerà dal letto, seminuda e dolcissima, confusa nel chiarore.
La seguiranno col fiato sospeso gli dei del cordoglio e dell'ira,
la sbircerà fra le ciglia il povero Epimeteo, l'abbagliato,
e sulle vette del Caucaso le aquile
solleveranno i loro becchi insanguinati. Vai, ragazza,
dice l'alba che arriva leggera, una seconda volta
e non temere, guarda come la luce
circonda ora la terra, è una carezza, e tu continui, con pazienza
avvicinati a te stessa, a quel destino che salva
o che condanna. Lo sai : TOMORROW IS NOW, per te e per tutti.

Babele dorme, sogna nelle sue lingue la gioia intraducibile.

PROSPECT HILL

Sull'orlo di una collina che immagino bassa,
con gli occhi perduti nei gomitoli del verde
o del traffico: è così che trascorri i tuoi giorni?
Anche tu persa, mi dici, reclusa
senza colpa fra matasse di farmaci e di fumo,
residuo umano d'umana storia che conduce
a un luogo dove io non sarò mai, il Connecticut,
che scatta come lama di coltello

Fingers like butterflies
run over the chords of many guitars, strange languages
intersect, bicker and rub together, songs
pass slow or fast across the skies, the wine is good.
Now we are sitting on a bridge between invisible banks,
above a river that sparkles and sings, and we smile.

Tomorrow, shortly before dawn, when the fish rise
and dart silvery over the water, with a wing-beat Pandora
will slip out of bed, half-naked, supremely sweet, confused in the
                                                      brightness.
With bated breath the gods of grief and wrath will follow her,
poor Epimetheus, dazzled, will squint out at her,
and on the summits of the Caucasus the eagles
will raise their bloodied beaks. Rise up, girl,
a second time, says the dawn arriving lightly,
and do not fear, see how light
now surrounds the earth in a caress and go on with patience,
draw close to yourself, to the destiny that saves
or condemns. As you know: TOMORROW IS NOW, for you and all of us.

Babel sleeps, dreaming in its tongues of joy untranslatable.

PROSPECT HILL

On the brow of a hill I imagine to be low,
gaze lost in the tangles of greenery
or traffic: is this how you while away your days?
You too lost, you tell me, shut away
guiltless in a shambles of drugs and smoke,
human remnant of a human story that leads
to a place I shall never visit, Connecticut,
a name which jerks like the blade of a knife

quando canta furiosa
sulla gola o sul cuore delle vittime, sui seni.
Sono un ostaggio, scrivi,
*ogni fuga è impossibile ormai
da questa gabbia bipolare. Non concede
più nulla nessun'alba a nessun fiore. Prigionia.
Se fosse amico il re dell'universo...* Ah, ma tu questo
lo sai fin troppo bene, invano i passi
percorrono la sala delle udienze, mentre sopra i lontani
contrafforti Appalachi scende il primo
gelo azzurro d'ottobre. Invece credo
che in questi mesi autunnali dentro i tuoi cieli
passino alti i pivieri dorati del Pacifico
diretti verso sud, per diecimila
chilometri di volo.
Se, come spero, li vedi, e se ascolti
i loro gridi lunghi, lamentosi,
se un'ombra corre la tua collina e poi scompare,
seguili con la mente, va con il loro andare finché puoi,
se ti sostiene il fiato, il sogno o il vento.
Volano con la luce sopra i baratri
più profondi del mare.

STORIE DELL'ARMADILLO

Buongiorno, dice l'armadillo a un netturbino. Per caso
ha visto passare di qui un opossum?
L'uomo alza la scopa verso nord, dove una nube
fluttua sopra i deserti come una grande
montagna. L'armadillo
ringrazia e s'incammina controvento.

*

when it sings furious
on the throat or heart of its victims, on their breasts.
I am a hostage, you write,
all flight is impossible now
from this bipolar cage. It no longer allows
any dawn to any flower. Imprisonment.
If only the king of the universe were my friend... Ah, but this
you know only too well, steps
pace the courtroom in vain, while over the distant
spurs of the Appalachians descends the first
light blue frost of October. I believe, though,
that during these autumn months Pacific golden plovers
pass high across your skies
flying south, eight thousand miles.
If, as I hope, you see them, and if you hear
their long lamenting cries,
if a shadow falls across your hill then moves on,
follow it in your mind, go with them as far as you can,
if breath, dream or wind sustains you.
They fly with the light above chasms
deeper than the sea.

STORIES OF THE ARMADILLO

Good morning, says the armadillo to a street-sweeper.
Have you seen an opossum pass this way at all?
The man raises his broom to the north, where a cloud
floats over the desert like a great
mountain. The armadillo
thanks him and trundles off into the wind.

*

Addosso la corazza e l'elmo in testa: così va
con la sua vista scarsa e le sue carni
deliziose e protette. Va perché va,
perché bisogna andare, perché il mondo
è grande, il tempo breve. Poi il profumo
di certi fiori, davvero delizioso.

*

L'armadillo canticchia sul cammino.
Non lo ascolta nessuno.
È un peccato: se qualcuno lo sentisse
potremmo sapere cosa canta
questo piccolo animale coraggioso. Magari
ci metteremmo in cammino anche noi.

*

Adesso l'armadillo ha sete: è in mezzo al deserto.
Segue ancora le tracce dell'opossum, ma il deserto
non conserva le tracce. Allora segue
certe linee più scure sul terreno e così arriva
davanti a un carro armato rimasto lì nel nulla.
Salve, dice l'armadillo al carro armato.
Ma quello resta zitto.

*

Se il carro armato potesse pensare,
forse sarebbe stupido. Invece è vuoto,
arrugginito e impolverato. Ma l'armadillo è cocciuto.
Lei è grande e grosso, gli dice. Ma non parla, non saluta.
Dovrò morire di sete davanti a un maleducato?
Per fortuna dalla mestizia del cannone
sbuca adagio un topino.
Non badarci, gli fa. Questo è un disadattato.

Clad in armour and helmet: off he goes
with his feeble vision and tasty
well-protected flesh. He goes because he goes,
because one has to go, because the world
is vast, time short. Then the scent
of certain flowers… a real delight.

*

The armadillo hums a tune as he goes.
No one listens.
A pity: if someone heard him
we would know what this plucky
little creature sings about. We might even
venture forth ourselves.

*

Now the armadillo is thirsty: he's in the middle of the desert.
Still following the tracks of the opossum, but
its tracks are lost in the desert. So he follows
some darker marks in the sand and comes
to an army tank abandoned there in the back of beyond.
Hi there, says the armadillo.
But the tank makes no reply.

*

If the tank could think,
it might be amazed. In fact it is empty,
rusty and covered in dust. But the armadillo is obstinate.
You are big and strong, he says. But you don't speak, nor even say hello.
Must I die of thirst because you are so boorish?
Fortunately a mouse emerges slowly
from the decrepitude of the barrel.
Don't take any notice, she says. He's a freak.

Vieni dentro, ti offro qualcosa.
E l'armadillo ringrazia.

*

Quando è necessario
l'armadillo può scavare per ore:
lunghe tane, zone umide e buie dove aspettare
tempi migliori, piogge, epoche in cui la speranza
non è poi del tutto impossibile. L'attesa
sia pure lunga, lui la inganna dormendo.
E quando sorge la luna legge Cervantes.

*

In uno stato quasi del nord hanno fatto una legge
sugli armadilli: è vietato possederne.
Si possono possedere
automobili, schiavi in maschera, fucili, ma armadilli
proprio no. È una legge interessante,
pensa l'armadillo. E si ferma un po'
in quello stato
così lungimirante.

*

Certe volte, in sogno, gli sembra di vederli:
branchi di puma, giaguari, altri animali forti
di cui non sa il nome. Colonne di autotreni,
ruote larghe, dentate, selvaggina
ignara di un'estinzione immensa.
Predatori, disperati, fuggiaschi,
tutti in fila nella stessa direzione, tutti
ugualmente entusiasti.
Allora si sveglia e pensa.

*

Come inside and I'll get you something.
And the armadillo thanks her.

    *

When necessary
the armadillo can dig for hours:
long burrows, dark damp places in which to await
better days, rain, times when hope
is not completely impossible. However long
the wait, he kills the time in sleep.
And when the moon rises reads Cervantes.

    *

In a northernish state they have made a law
on armadillos: owning one is forbidden.
You can own cars, slaves in fancy dress, guns, but armadillos
definitely not. An interesting law,
thinks the armadillo. And he stays a while
in a state
so forward-looking.

    *

Sometimes, in his dreams, he seems to see
prides of pumas, jaguars, other mighty animals
of name unknown to him. Columns of lorries,
wide, cogged wheels, game
unaware of an immense extinction.
Predators, fugitives, no-hopers,
all strung out in the same direction, all
equally enthusiastic.
Then he wakes up and thinks.

    *

Uno dice: l'armadillo (adesso sta pensando). Ma in effetti
l'armadillo è un concetto teorico: una specie
o comunque una categoria. Io non sono
l'armadillo, sono un armadillo, e non so nulla
di quello che sto facendo. Il mio futuro
è modesto: qualche insetto, lumache,
magari dei figli : quattro,
uno per ogni punto cardinale.
Eppure i miei passi vaghi
vanno da qualche parte, queste tane che scavo
serviranno anche ad altri, con un po' di fortuna. Lo spazio
serberà qualche traccia del mio fantasticare
controcorrente. Così l'armadillo, l'idea
di armadillo, mi guida, e io guido lei, io la conduco
nel mio piccolo verso i tempi a venire e le montagne
gelate, e i grandi laghi.

*

Quando si lucida le scaglie, si fa bello
l'armadillo ripensa alla figura improbabile
di un certo suo antenato italiano :
quello che venne esposto
insieme a un unicorno, a un vitello marino
e a certi coccodrilli scorticati
da un signore padano insieme ai resti
dei nemici prima uccisi e poi mummificati.
Pare ci fosse anche un drago a sette teste : non stupisce
l'astuzia dei potenti, né l'orgoglio
di quel collezionista. Ma da dove
poteva mai venire un armadillo
nel Trecento alla palude dei Gonzaga? Una leggenda,
senz'altro, o forse un'acquisizione
posteriore. Ne discende:
che alla bacheca dell'orrore è preferibile il charango
(mal che vada, è pur musica, non incubi) ; che i serpenti

People say: *the* armadillo (now he is thinking). But actually
the armadillo is a theoretical concept: a species
or at any rate a category. I am not
the armadillo, I'm *an* armadillo, and I've no idea
what I am really doing. My future
is modest: the odd insect, snails,
possible children: four of them,
one for each point of the compass.
Yet my uncertain steps
are leading somewhere, these burrows I dig
will also serve others, with a bit of luck. Space
will preserve some trace of my countercultural
daydreaming. So *the* armadillo, the idea
of armadillo, guides me, and I guide it, I lead it
in my own small way towards the days to come and the icy
mountains, and the great lakes.

*

When he polishes his scales, smartens up,
the armadillo reconsiders the unlikely figure
of an Italian ancestor of his,
who was exposed
in the company of a unicorn, a sea calf
and some flayed crocodiles
by a Po Valley tyrant, together with the remains
of his enemies, first murdered then mummified.
Apparently there was also a seven-headed dragon: nothing surprising
about the guile of the powerful, nor the pride
of that collector. But how
could an armadillo have possibly come
to the Gonzaga marshes in the thirteen hundreds? A legend,
of course, or maybe a later
acquisition. It follows that:
the charango is preferable to a showcase of horrors
(when all's said and done, it is at least music, not nightmares);

sono sempre esistiti; che un armadillo, come ogni ribelle,
deve fare molta attenzione.

*

Quello che gli piace: l'acqua, il vento
se non è troppo forte, i boschi, l'erba magnifica
quando è umida di notte e annuncia l'alba,
l'odore di funghi e certi insetti
delicati. Anche in città ci sono posti mica male :
vicoli, tubi, cantine qualche volta. E nessun puma.
Venera inoltre la pacifica
tenacia dell'opossum: l'indifeso.

*

Si può dire: il bardato, il cingolato, il solitario,
lo sdentato, il pavido, il lento,
quello che non può saltare, che non si gira,
il mangiavermi, il leccaformiche, il ladro,
il fuggiasco, il talpone che gira in tondo,
il tiratardi, il nottambulo, l'unghiaforte;
quello che si diverte a far cadere i cavalli,
li azzoppa e si squassa le scaglie
dal ridere dentro il suo buco graveolente.
Lo si può maledire, cercare di notte
con bastoni appuntiti, o con mazze, denti di cane.
Si possono reclutare indigeni ubriachi
o eserciti di zanzare per dargli la caccia.
L'armadillo non ci bada

*

È inutile tirarlo per la coda:
come si sa per esperienza l'armadillo non cede
così facilmente. E poi ci sono voluti
forse cinquanta milioni di anni, un imprevisto
casuale e un bel po' di fortuna:

snakes have always existed; an armadillo, like any rebel,
must be very careful.

*

The things he likes: water, the wind
if not too strong, woods, grass magnificent
when it is damp at night and heralds the dawn,
the smell of mushrooms and certain delicate
insects. In town, too, there are some quite decent places:
alleys, pipes, cellars sometimes. And no pumas.
He also venerates the peaceful
tenacity of the opossum: the defenceless one.

*

You could describe him as: caparisoned, caterpillar-tracked, solitary,
toothless, timorous, slow,
incapable of jumping, or turning around,
worm-eater, ant-licker, thief,
fugitive, big revolving mole,
slowcoach, sleep-walker, mighty-claws;
his idea of fun is to fell horses:
he lames them and bursts his scales
laughing inside his foul-smelling hole.
You can curse him, track him at night
with pointed sticks, clubs or toothy dogs.
You can recruit drunken natives
or armies of mosquitos to hunt him.
The armadillo doesn't care.

*

There's no point pulling him by the tail:
experience teaches that the armadillo does not give in
so easily. After all, it has taken
maybe fifty million years, a chance
event and a good dose of luck:

un marinaio di belle speranze,
una tempesta, un naufragio in un golfo terribile,
una terra fiorita e ignara cui approdare.
Ne ha viste troppe per spaventarsi o perdere coraggio.
È stato lungo il cammino, arduo il viaggio.
Ora procede, un passo dopo l'altro. Quasi allegro.

*

Tra le altre cose che ha riportato su dai tempi
più lontani, anche la lebbra. La conosce, ne sa
l'obbrobrio, l'umiltà delle carni corrose,
e quanto è fragile la corazza dell'orgoglio.
Così saluta ogni fiore che incontra, gentilmente,
e ai desolati porta farfalle secche, piccoli doni.

*

Un punto debole, certo: il solletico. Sotto la coda,
dove molle si snoda il ventre, e le antiche
dolcezze si accampano,
basta poco, piuma morbida o carezza,
pennacchio, cima d'aconito. Subito scoppia il riso
irrefrenabile. Ride l'armadillo mentre mani
lo trascinano indietro, verso morte o prigionia, verso il fatidico
bastone che lo attende. Eppure ride,
e non è solo questione di solletico. Pensare
a tutto questo odio, alla violenza, alla brama,
e a ogni cosa in fin dei conti ridicola, perduta
nel nulla delle epoche, scaglietta di storia
nella lorica di storie che la fame o la forza s'intessono,
uguali sempre, sempre dimenticabili, inutili
atrocità ferruginose. Quando ride così,
l'armadillo non fa
propriamente paura: sconcerto, forse, negli occhi di chi
si accanisce, s'infervora. Appetito che scema, e improvviso
una specie di vuoto allo stomaco: mediocre

a sailor with high hopes,
a storm, a shipwreck in a terrible bay,
a blooming, unsuspecting land on which to come ashore.
He has seen too much to panic or lose courage.
The way has been long, the journey arduous.
Now he goes on, step by step. Almost happy.

*

Another thing he has brought with him
from the distant past: leprosy. He knows it, knows
the stigma, the shame of corroded flesh,
and how fragile is the armour of pride.
So he greets every flower he meets, with courtesy,
and to the desolate brings dried butterflies, little gifts.

*

One weak point, of course: he's ticklish. Under the tail,
where the soft underbelly begins, seat
of age-old pleasures,
it takes very little, a soft feather or caress,
quill or wolfsbane tip, to provoke an outburst of irrepressible
laughter. The armadillo laughs as hands
drag him backwards, towards death or detention, the fateful
club that awaits him. Even so he laughs,
and its not just the tickling, but thinking
of all this hatred, violence, greed,
and everything ultimately ridiculous, lost
in the vacuity of the ages, tiny segment of history
in the corselet of stories woven by hunger and brute force,
always the same, always forgettable, pointless
ferruginous atrocities. When he laughs in this way,
the armadillo does not really instil fear:
unease, possibly, in the eyes of the
ruthless, fanatical persecutor. Loss of appetite and a sudden
void in the stomach as the mediocrity

chiama una biologia rassegnata, senza sogni, una politica
medicamentosa, sordida,
la coscienza ne ride, cupamente,
e chi assiste alla scena s'adombra, s'inquieta.
Non è un bello spettacolo,
un armadillo che ride morendo
mentre sdrucciola. In realtà,
con la strana allegria delle prede,
lui guarda in quegli istanti dentro gli occhi
del gliptodonte, e gli parla,
come talvolta si parla a un amico o a un fratello scomparsi,
eppure sempre presenti,
e spiritosi.

of a resigned biology is revealed, the lack of vision of a sordid
sticking-plaster politics,
conscience laughs, darkly,
and the onlooker is disturbed and troubled.
It's not a pretty sight
an armadillo laughing as it is dragged
to its death. In fact,
with the strange euphoria of the victim,
he gazes during those moments into the eyes
of the glyptodont, and speaks to him,
as you might speak to a friend
or a brother who have died
but are still present,
and amusing.

NOTES

p. 43 'Crespi d'Adda': The name of a model village, near Lecco, founded in 1878 by the textile entrepreneur Cristoforo Benigno Crespi to house his workers.

p. 51 'Vatel': We have little information about the suicide of one of France's greatest cooks; of the very few accounts, two deliciously cynical letters by Mme. de Sévigné (dated 24 and 26 April 1671) are extant. The epigraph is taken from one of them.

p. 53 'Continente': the name of a vast new shopping complex in Portugal.

p. 69 'Tremor (II) ' : Like zio (uncle) Lampo, Radamès and Rigoletto were real people. Rigoletto was so called, apparently, because his birth, no doubt untimely and inconvenient, occurred during the interval of a performance of Verdi's opera of that name, at which his music-loving parent was present. I have no information about Radamès. But this all refers to the early years of the twentieth century.

p. 83 'Letter from Nikolajevka': Fabio Pusterla's father, though living in Switzerland, enlisted in the Italian army as a young man and was sent to fight in Russia. He was one of the few Alpini to escape the massacre at Nikolajevka in 1943.

p. 85 'Deposition': The reference is to a "Deposition of Christ" by the Florentine Mannerist painter Pontormo, which combines emotional intensity and elegance, the figures piled into the picture space with an intentional lack of logic.

p. 99 'April 2006: Postcards of Italy': In the general election of 9 / 10 April 2006, a majority of Italians living abroad, who had acquired the right to vote in 2001 as a result of a law enacted by the political right, voted for Romano Prodi's centre-left coalition, tipping the balance in favour of the left.

p. 107 'Letters from Babel': Babel is also the name of a literary translation festival held in Bellinzona. In the year in question, it featured writers from the former Yugoslavia.

p. 113 'Stories of the Armadillo': The poet writes: "The idea that the armadillo, like the opossum before it, is working its way up the American continent towards Canada, in the opposite direction to the great migrations of predators during the Miocene Period, comes from the penetrating writings of S. J. Gould, which stimulated my imagination when I read them many years ago.

From subsequent research, I have gathered details and curiosities regarding the life of the armadillo and its slow but irresistible march northwards, believed to have begun with a shipwreck off Florida, an area to which the few specimens being transported by a sailor adapted perfectly, reproducing and making their way into the undergrowth. In addition to a few scientific writings and miscellaneous information gathered from the internet (including the fact that the State of Maine has a law banning its citizens from owning an armadillo; and the information, deriving from the fantastic diaries of an eighteenth-century traveller, that the Gonzaga family's famous gallery or horrors included an armadillo), I have drawn particularly on the observations contained in *Pampa, Tierra afuera e Tierra Adentro*, edited by G. Guadalupi (Rome, 1991), which I owe to my friends Dan, Patrizia and Danilo.

I began writing these 'Stories of the Armadillo' purely for fun. And the matter would probably have gone no further but for the enthusiasm of the fifth-year pupils at Lugano Cassarate primary school and, above all, the encouragement of another friend, Oscar, who urged me to continue the game more seriously. To them I dedicate these poems.

Going by recent sightings, which are difficult to verify, a number of specimens have been spotted in the vicinity of Boston, and also in southern Indiana – news which I find truly comforting.

Finally, we cannot exclude the possibility that some readers may be tempted to read these notes, and the Stories of the Armadillo as a whole, in a vaguely allegorical way. If so, how could the author deny such an eventuality?

Run, armadillo, run!"

BIOGRAPHICAL NOTES

FABIO PUSTERLA was born in Mendrisio in 1957. A graduate in modern literature at the University of Pavia, he works in Lugano (Switzerland), teaching at the local high school and at the university, and lives across the border in Valsolda, in Como province (Italy).

As well as many essays on linguistic and literary topics, he has published *Cultura e linguaggio della Valle Intelvi* (in collaboration with Claudia Patocchi, Senna Comasco, 1983), and an anthology entitled *Lombardia* (in collaboration with Angelo Stella and Cesare Repossi, La Scuola, Brescia, 1990). He has also edited a critical edition of the narrative works of Vittorio Imbriani for the Fondazione Bembo (3 vols., Longanesi-Guanda, Milan, 1992-1994).

His translations include four collections of poems by Philippe Jaccottet (*Il Barbagianni. L'Ignorante*, with an essay by Jean Starobinski, Einaudi, Turin, 1992; *Alla luce d'inverno. Pensieri sotto le nuvole*, Marcos y Marcos, Milan, 1997), and other verses collected together in *Edera e calce* (Ancona, 1995). Also by Jaccottet, he has translated prose pieces relating to travel in Italy, contained in *Libretto* (Scheiwiller, Milan, 1995), the volume *Paesaggi con figure assenti* (Dadò, Coll. CH, Locarno, 1996) and the essay *Austria* (Bollati Boringhieri, Turin, 2003). He has also translated and written a preface to the novel *Adagio* by the Portuguese writer Nuno Judice (Ripatransone, Sestante, 1994), and various prose pieces and poems by Yves Bonnefoy, Nicolas Bouvier, André Frénaud, Maurice Chappaz, Corinna Bille, Eugenio De Andrade and Daniel De Roulet, which have appeared in reviews or anthologies. For his work as a translator, he won the Premio Prezzolini in 1994. He has edited an anthology of contemporary French poetry, *Nel pieno giorno dell'oscurità* (Marcos y Marcos, Milan, 2000), and *Cento piccole storie crudeli* by Corinne Bille (Casagrande, Bellinzona, 2001).

His volumes of poetry include *Concessione all'inverno* (Casagrande, Bellinzona, 1985, for which he was awarded the Premio Montale and the Premio Schiller; 2nd ed. 2000), *Bocksten* (Marcos y Marcos, Milan, 1989), *Le cose senza storia* (*ibid.*, 1994, for which he received the Premio Hermann Ganz and the Premio Valle del Metauro 1994); *Isla Persa* (I semi del salice, Locarno 1998), *Laghi e oltre* (with Alida Airaghi and Anna Felder, Lietocollelibri,

1999), *Pietra Sangue* (Marcos y Marcos, Milan, 1999; Premio Schiller 2000; finalist Premio Viareggio 2000); and the "plaquettes" *Sotto il giardino* (with French and German versions, Lausanne, 1992), *Tra la terra e il cielo* (with Antonio Rossi and Francesco Scarabicchi, engravings by Alberto Rocco and an introduction by Massimo Raffaelli), *Danza macabra* (Lietocollelibri, 1995) and *Bandiera di carta* (published by Fabrizio Mugnaini, Scandicci, 1996). More recent is the *Livre d'artiste Pietre*, produced in collaboration with the artist Massimo Cavalli and published by Sassello di Novazzano (2000).

In 2002, he published the brief sylloge *Ipotesi sui castori*, for Flussi editions of Valmadrera, edited by Vincenzo Girelli, followed in 2003 by *Sette frammenti della terra di nessuno* (*ibid.*), subsequently collected together in the volume *Folla sommersa* (Marcos y Marcos, Milan, 2004). His essays on education, *Una giocca di splendore* (Casagrande, Bellinzona) appeared in 2008. The anthology *Le terre emerse. Poesia 1985-2008* (Einaudi, Turin) was published in 2009, and a year later the collection *Corpo stellare* (Marcos y Marcos, 2010) appeared. Both books have won several prizes, the Einaudi anthology the Premio Dessì in 2009 and *Corpo stellare* the Premio Schiller and the Premio Ceppo Pistoia, both in 2011. Fabio Pusterla was awarded the Premio Gottfried Keller for lifetime achievement in 2007.

His works have also been published in French: (*Une voix pour le noir*, translated by Mathilde Vischer, preface by Philippe Jaccottet, Ed. D'En Bas, Lausanne, 2001; *Deux Rives*, translated by Philippe Jaccottet and Béatrice de Jurquet, Cheynes, 2002; *Les choses sans histoire*, translated by Mathilde Vischer, Empreintes, Lausanne, 2003; *Ultimes paysages*, translated by Eric Dazzan, L'arrière-Pays, 2009); in German (*So lange Zeit bleibt / Dum vacat*, translated by Hanno Helbling, afterword by Massimo Raffaeli, Limmat Verlag, Zurich, 2002; *Bocksten*, translated by J. Aerne, Limmat Verlag, Zurich, 2010); in Serbian (*Stvari bez istorije*, translated by Dejan Illic, Belgrade, 2002; *Folla sommersa*, translated by Dejan Illic, Belgrade, 2007); and Spanish (*Bocksten*, translated by Di Rafael-José Diaz, Qualea, Torrelavega, 2008). Many individual poems have appeared in translation in reviews or anthologies in the main European languages.

SIMON KNIGHT was born in Bishop's Stortford in 1948 and studied Modern Languages (Italian and French) at Trinity Hall, Cambridge. His studies included periods in Florence and Monza. He now lives partly in the UK, partly in Parma, Italy.

After teacher training, he spent seven years as a teacher of English as a foreign language in Madagascar. On returning to England in 1981, he started working as a freelance translator, while maintaining an interest in education as parent, teacher and trustee of a Christian school, which he founded with a group of friends in 1989.

As a translator, he has specialised in the media and arts, developing a special interest in Italian-speaking Switzerland. He also worked for many years as a public-service interpreter.

His literary translation activities began as a 'sideline', when he was first asked to translate some poems by Fabio Pusterla in 1999. The project grew and has enjoyed support from the Swiss Arts Council Pro Helvetia. He now takes a special interest in writers from Italian-speaking Switzerland and is currently translating a Ticino 'classic': *Il fondo del sacco* (1970) by Plinio Martini.

ALAN BROWNJOHN, poet, novelist, children's writer and critic was born in London in 1931. He was educated at Merton College, Oxford and worked as a schoolteacher until 1965 and then as a lecturer at Battersea College of Education and South Bank Polytechnic until he left to become a full-time freelance writer in 1979. A regular broadcaster, reviewer and contributor to journals including the *Times Literary Supplement*, *Encounter* and the *Sunday Times*, Alan Brownjohn was poetry critic for the *New Statesman* and was Chairman of the Poetry Society between 1982 and 1988. He has also served on the Arts Council literature panel, was a Labour councillor and a candidate for Parliament. His first collection of poetry, *The Railings*, was published in 1961. Other poetry books include *Collected Poems 1952-1983* (1983, re-issued in 1988) and *The Observation Car* (1990). He is also the author of three novels, *The Way You Tell Them: A Yarn of the*

Nineties (1990), *The Long Shadows* (1997) and *A Funny Old Year* (2001), as well as two books for children and a critical study of the poet Philip Larkin. His novel *Windows on the Moon* was published in 2009. His latest poetry collection *Ludbrooke & Others* was published by Enitharmon in July 2010.

Alan Brownjohn received the Writers' Guild's Lifetime Achievement Award in 2007.

Also available in the Arc Publications
'VISIBLE POETS' SERIES (Series Editor: Jean Boase-Beier)

No. 1 – MIKLÓS RADNÓTI (Hungary)
Camp Notebook
Translated by Francis Jones, introduced by George Szirtes

No. 2 – BARTOLO CATTAFI (Italy)
Anthracite
Translated by Brian Cole, introduced by Peter Dale
(Poetry Book Society Recommended Translation)

No. 3 – MICHAEL STRUNGE (Denmark)
A Virgin from a Chilly Decade
Translated by Bente Elsworth, introduced by John Fletcher

No. 4 – TADEUSZ RÓZEWICZ (Poland)
recycling
Translated by Barbara Bogoczek (Plebanek) & Tony Howard,
introduced by Adam Czerniawski

No. 5 – CLAUDE DE BURINE (France)
Words Have Frozen Over
Translated by Martin Sorrell, introduced by Susan Wicks

No. 6 – CEVAT ÇAPAN (Turkey)
Where Are You, Susie Petschek?
Translated by Cevat Çapan & Michael Hulse,
introduced by A. S. Byatt

No. 7 – JEAN CASSOU (France)
33 Sonnets of the Resistance
With an original introduction by Louis Aragon
Translated by Timothy Adès, introduced by Alistair Elliot

No. 8 – ARJEN DUINKER (Holland)
The Sublime Song of a Maybe
Translated by Willem Groenewegen, introduced by Jeffrey Wainwright

No. 9 – MILA HAUGOVÁ (Slovakia)
Scent of the Unseen
Translated by James & Viera Sutherland-Smith,
introduced by Fiona Sampson

No. 10 – ERNST MEISTER (Germany)
Between Nothing and Nothing
Translated by Jean Boase-Beier, introduced by John Hartley Williams

No. 11 – YANNIS KONDOS (Greece)
Absurd Athlete
Translated by David Connolly, introduced by David Constantine

No. 12 – BEJAN MATUR (Turkey)
In the Temple of a Patient God
Translated by Ruth Christie, introduced by Maureen Freely

No. 13 – GABRIEL FERRATER (Catalonia / Spain)
Women and Days
Translated by Arthur Terry, introduced by Seamus Heaney

No. 14 – INNA LISNIANSKAYA (Russia)
Far from Sodom
Translated by Daniel Weissbort, introduced by Elaine Feinstein
(Poetry Book Society Recommended Translation)

No. 15 – SABINE LANGE (Germany)
The Fishermen Sleep
Translated by Jenny Williams, introduced by Mary O'Donnell

No. 16 – TAKAHASHI MUTSUO (Japan)
We of Zipangu
Translated by James Kirkup & Tamaki Makoto, introduced by Glyn Pursglove

No. 17 – JURIS KRONBERGS (Latvia)
Wolf One-Eye
Translated by Mara Rozitis, introduced by Jaan Kaplinski

No. 18 – REMCO CAMPERT (Holland)
I Dreamed in the Cities at Night
Translated by Donald Gardner, introduced by Paul Vincent

No. 19 – DOROTHEA ROSA HERLIANY (Indonesia)
Kill the Radio
Translated by Harry Aveling, introduced by Linda France

No. 20 – SOLEÏMAN ADEL GUÉMAR (Algeria)
State of Emergency
Translated by Tom Cheesman & John Goodby, introduced by Lisa Appignanesi
(PEN Translation Award)

No. 21 – ELI TOLARETXIPI (Spain / Basque)
Still Life with Loops
Translated by Philip Jenkins, introduced by Robert Crawford

No. 22 – FERNANDO KOFMAN (Argentina)
The Flights of Zarza
Translated by Ian Taylor, introduced by Andrew Graham Yooll

No. 23 – LARISSA MILLER (Russia)
Guests of Eternity
Translated by Richard McKane, introduced by Sasha Dugdale
(Poetry Book Society Recommended Translation)

No. 24 – ANISE KOLTZ (Luxembourg)
At the Edge of Night
Translated by Anne-Marie Glasheen, introduced by Caroline Price

No. 25 – MAURICE CARÊME (Belgium)
Defying Fate
Translated by Christopher Pilling, introduced by Martin Sorrell

No. 26 – VALÉRIE ROUZEAU (France)
Cold Spring in Winter
Translated by Susan Wicks, introduced by Stephen Romer
(Short-listed for Griffin Poetry Prize, 2010 &
Oxford-Weidenfeld Translation Prize, 2010)

No. 27 – RAZMIK DAVOYAN (France)
Whispers and Breath of the Meadows
Translated by Arminé Tamrazian, introduced by W. N. Herbert

No. 28 – FRANÇOIS JACQMIN (Belgium)
The Book of the Snow
Translated by Philip Mosley, introduced by Clive Scott
(Short-listed for Griffin Poetry Prize, 2011)

No. 29 – KRISTIINA EHIN (Estonia)
The Scent of Your Shadow
Translated by Ilmar Lehtpere, introduced by Sujata Bhatt
(Poetry Book Society Recommended Translation)

No. 30 – META KUŠAR (Slovenia)
Ljubljana
Translated by Ana Jelnikar & Stephen Watts, introduced by Francis R. Jones

No. 31 – LUDWIG STEINHERR (Germany)
Before the Invention of Paradise
Translated by Richard Dove, introduced by Jean Boase-Beier